Curiosities Unleashed: A Journey Through Astonishing Facts

Ryan Hake

INTRODUCTION

Curious Heart invites you on an extraordinary journey that will take you to the world's secret places and beyond. Curiosity Revealed: Journey to Ultimate Truth is more than a book; This is the greatest treasure trove of incredible, fascinating, and terrifying facts the world and the entire world has to offer. From the deepest oceans to the brightest stars, from the past to the future, we will discover wonders and mysteries that fuel our endless curiosity. Why did we start this way? Because curiosity is in human nature. It allows us to ask questions, seek answers, and wonder about the breadth and complexity of our lives. This book is a celebration of the constant pursuit of knowledge; It is a curiosity designed to surprise, inspire, and motivate. Each chapter is a door to a new area of discovery. We'll uncover strange animal behavior that defies logic, magnificent architecture that proves human ingenuity, and groundbreaking science that challenges our understanding of reality. We will delve into the annals of history to uncover the secrets of the past, delving into areas of cultural curiosity and celebrating the diversity of presentation. But Curiosity Unleashed is more than a collection of facts. It invites us to look at the world with curiosity and reminds us that no matter how much we learn, the universe is always more mysterious than we think. This is a call to wonder, to ask questions, to explore the wonderful world we call home. So, dear readers, whether you are a lifelong learner, a passionate hobbyist, or simply looking for a spark for your idea, you have come to the right place. Prepare to be amazed, laugh, wonder, and maybe even be confused. Most importantly, prepare to remember the joy and wonder that comes with exploring the unknown. Welcome to "Curiosity Revealed". Let the journey begin.

Chapter 1: Wonders of the Natural World

-**Section 1.1**: Bizarre Animal Behaviors

 - Examples of unusual animal habits and the scientific explanations behind them.

-**Section 1.2**: Astonishing Plant Life

- Exploration of extraordinary plants and their survival mechanisms.

-**Section 1.3**: Mysteries of the Oceans

- Deep-sea discoveries and unusual marine life forms.

 Chapter 2: Phenomenal Human Achievements

-**Section 2.1**: Architectural Marvels

 - Stories behind the world's most iconic buildings and structures.

 - **Section 2.2**: Record-Breaking Feats

 - A look at extraordinary human records in sports, science, and endurance.

 - **Section 2.3**: Innovations that Changed the World

 - How certain inventions have shaped modern society.

-Chapter 6: Puzzles of the Universe

-Section 6.1: Cosmic Mysteries

- Discussing unexplained phenomena in the universe.

-Section 6.2: Theories of Time and Space

- Exploring concepts that challenge our understanding of reality.

-Section 6.3: Future Technologies and Exploration

- Speculating on the future of human technology and space travel.

Chapter 1:<u>Wonders of the Natural Word</u>

List of 100 facts about unusual animal habits along with their scientific explanations.

1. **Turritopsis dohrnii (Immortal Jellyfish) Rejuvenation**: This jellyfish can revert to its juvenile form after reaching maturity, potentially living forever under laboratory conditions, a process related to cellular transdifferentiation.

2. **Capuchin Monkeys Use Tools**: In Brazil, capuchin monkeys have been observed using stones as tools to crack nuts, showing advanced problem-solving abilities and tool-use behavior.

3. **Dolphins Name Themselves**: Dolphins emit unique whistles that may function as names, allowing individual identification among peers, a complex communication skill demonstrating self-awareness.

4. **Elephants Mourning**: Elephants show behaviors resembling mourning, such as lingering around the bodies of deceased herd members, suggesting a deep sense of loss and social connections.

5. **Crows Hold Funerals**: Crows gather around their dead to learn about dangers and potentially alert others of threats, indicating complex social behavior and learning.

6. **Bees Dance to Communicate**: Honeybees perform a "waggle dance" to communicate the location of food sources to hive mates, a sophisticated form of communication involving direction and distance.

7. **Ants Farm Aphids**: Some ant species protect and care for aphids to harvest their honeydew, a mutualistic relationship where ants get food and aphids receive protection.

8. **Octopuses Dream and Change Color**: Octopuses have been observed changing colors while sleeping, suggesting they may dream, highlighting their complex brain function and neural mechanisms.

9. **Lyrebirds Mimic Chainsaws**: The superb lyrebird can mimic natural and artificial sounds, including chainsaws and camera shutters, a remarkable example of vocal learning and environmental adaptation.

10. **Pufferfish Create Art**: Male pufferfish create intricate patterns on the ocean floor as part of their mating ritual to attract females, demonstrating artistic behavior in fish.

This list is just the beginning, scratching the surface of the incredible behaviors animals have evolved. Each fact represents a story of adaptation, survival, and sometimes, sheer wonder, underlining the complexity and diversity of life on Earth.

11. **Archerfish Shoot Water to Hunt**: Archerfish can shoot jets of water at insects above the surface, knocking them into the water to eat. This behavior showcases remarkable precision and an understanding of water dynamics and refraction.

12. **Bowerbirds Build Decorative Nests**: Male bowerbirds construct elaborate and colorful nests, or "bowers," to attract females. This involves a sophisticated understanding of aesthetics and the use of objects to create visually appealing structures.

13. **Frogs Freeze for Winter**: Some frog species, like the wood frog, can freeze solid during winter and then thaw in spring, their bodies producing glucose as a natural antifreeze to protect vital organs.

14. **Humpback Whales Use Bubble Nets**: Humpback whales create "bubble nets" by blowing bubbles in a circle around their prey, trapping and concentrating the fish for easier feeding, demonstrating cooperative hunting tactics and spatial understanding.

15. **Mimic Octopus Changes Shape**: The mimic octopus can change its shape, color, and behavior to imitate more than 15 different species, including sea snakes and lionfish, as a defense mechanism against predators.

16. **Wolves Howl to Strengthen Social Bonds**: Wolves howl to communicate with their pack and assert territory. Howling also strengthens social bonds within the pack and can help to coordinate hunting strategies.

17. **Zebra Stripes as Insect Repellent**: The stripes of zebras may serve as a deterrent to biting insects like flies, which are less likely to land on striped surfaces, showcasing a natural adaptation to their environment.

18. **Pistol Shrimp Stun Prey with Bubbles**: The pistol shrimp can snap its claw shut so rapidly it creates a bubble that collapses to produce a loud noise and a shockwave, stunning its prey. This demonstrates an extraordinary use of physics in hunting.

19. **Draco Lizards Glide Using Winglike Flaps**: Draco lizards have extendable rib "wings" that allow them to glide from tree to tree in Southeast Asia's forests, an adaptation for mobility and escape from predators.

20. **Albatrosses Use Dynamic Soaring**: Albatrosses can travel vast distances with minimal energy by exploiting wind gradients over the ocean's surface, a behavior known as dynamic soaring. This technique showcases an advanced adaptation to their marine environment.

Each of these behaviors highlights the incredible adaptability and diversity of the animal kingdom, revealing how species have evolved unique solutions to survive and thrive in their respective environments.

21. **Vampire Bats Donate Blood**: Vampire bats will regurgitate blood to feed fellow bats who have failed to feed, demonstrating a rare form of altruism in the animal kingdom, crucial for colony survival.

22. **Sea Cucumbers Harden and Soften Their Bodies**: Sea cucumbers can change the stiffness of their bodies at will, using a unique protein to instantly harden their skin to protect against predators or soften it to squeeze through tight spaces.

23. **Salamanders Regenerate Lost Limbs**: Salamanders can fully regenerate lost limbs, tails, and even parts of their hearts and brains, showcasing remarkable cellular regeneration and reprogramming capabilities.

24. **Peacock Spiders Dance to Attract Mates**: Male peacock spiders perform elaborate dances with vibrant displays of their colorful abdomens to attract females, a complex ritual combining visual cues and vibration signals.

25. **Mantis Shrimp Punch**: The mantis shrimp strikes its prey with its claws at the speed of a bullet, generating both a shockwave and heat on impact, showcasing an extraordinary predatory technique.

26. **Giraffes Clean Their Ears with Their Tongues**: Giraffes have long tongues (up to 20 inches) that they use for feeding on leaves as well as for personal hygiene, such as cleaning their ears.

27. **Fireflies Synchronize Lights**: In certain areas, fireflies synchronize their light flashes in large groups, a phenomenon believed to help attract mates and a stunning example of collective behavior.

28. **Caterpillars Morph into Butterflies**: Through metamorphosis, caterpillars transform into butterflies, undergoing a complete physical reconstitution inside the chrysalis, a process that remains one of nature's most profound transformations.

29. **Penguins Propose with Pebbles**: Male penguins search the beach for the perfect pebble to present to their chosen mate. If the female accepts, it's used to build their nest, indicating a complex social and mating ritual.

30. **Elephant Seals Inhale Seawater to Clear Noses**: Elephant seals can suck in seawater and then forcefully expel it to clean out their nostrils, a necessary adaptation for an animal that spends much of its time diving deep underwater.

31. **Kangaroos Use Tail as Fifth Leg**: When walking slowly, kangaroos use their tail as a fifth leg to propel themselves forward, showcasing an unusual but efficient form of locomotion.

32. **Cuttlefish Use Dynamic Camouflage**: Cuttlefish can change their skin color and texture in seconds to blend into their surroundings, an advanced form of camouflage for hiding from predators or sneaking up on prey.

33. **Frigatebirds Sleep While Flying**: Frigatebirds can sleep while flying high in the sky, taking short naps with one-half of their brain at a time, a skill that allows them to stay airborne for weeks.

34. **Cats Bring Gifts to Teach Hunting**: Domestic cats often bring dead or injured prey back to their human caretakers, a behavior thought to be an extension of teaching their young how to hunt and eat.

35. **Orcas Use Tidal Waves to Hunt**: Orcas have been observed creating waves by swimming in unison to wash seals off ice floes, a sophisticated hunting strategy that demonstrates their ability to cooperate and plan.

36. **Tardigrades Survive in Space**: Tardigrades, or "water bears," can survive extreme conditions, including the vacuum of space, by entering a desiccated state known as cryptobiosis, showcasing extreme resilience.

37. **African Grey Parrots Understand Zero**: These parrots have demonstrated the ability to understand the concept of zero, an abstract notion that is a hallmark of advanced cognitive processing.

38. **Squirrels Fake Hide Their Nuts**: To deceive potential thieves, squirrels sometimes perform fake nut-burying actions, a behavior indicating an understanding of deception to protect their food sources.

39. **Dung Beetles Navigate by the Stars**: Dung beetles use the Milky Way as a navigation tool, the first known case of insects using the galaxy for orientation, showcasing a sophisticated natural GPS.

40. **Coral Spawning Events**: Many coral species simultaneously release eggs and sperm into the water on a single night each year, a synchronized event usually triggered by the moon, demonstrating an extraordinary level of coordination and timing.

41. **Hummingbirds Hover with Precision**: Hummingbirds can hover in mid-air thanks to their incredibly fast wing beats and rotating wing joints, allowing them to access nectar while expending minimal energy, an aerodynamic feat unmatched in the animal kingdom.

42. **Honeybees Make "Whoop" Sounds**: Recently discovered, honeybees emit a "whoop" sound when startled or when they bump into each other, suggesting a complex form of communication previously unknown.

43. **Goats Have Accents**: Goats can change their calls as they grow older and move into different social groups, suggesting that, like humans, they can develop 'accents' based on their social environment.

44. **Spiders Tune Their Webs**: Spiders can adjust the tension and stickiness of their webs, effectively 'tuning' them to alert to the presence and type of prey caught, a behavior that demonstrates an intricate understanding of their hunting tools.

45. **Glow-worms Illuminate to Attract Prey**: Glow-worms use bioluminescence to create light, attracting prey into their sticky web-like structures. This predatory tactic is a unique use of light in the natural world.

46. **Mudskippers Breathe Through Their Skin**: Mudskippers, a type of fish that can live on land, absorb oxygen through their skin and the lining of their mouth and throat, an adaptation that allows them to navigate terrestrial environments.

47. **Puffer Fish Inflate as Defense Mechanism**: When threatened, puffer fish inflate themselves by swallowing water or air, making them much larger and more difficult for predators to eat, a classic example of a physical defense mechanism.

48. **Desert Rain Frogs Squeal to Deter Predators**: The tiny desert rain frog emits a high-pitched squeal when threatened, a sound that is surprisingly menacing for such a small creature, serving as a deterrent to potential predators.

49. **Snow Leopards Use Their Tails as Blankets**: In the cold habitats they inhabit, snow leopards wrap their long, fluffy tails around their bodies and faces for warmth while sleeping, demonstrating an adaptive use of their physical traits.

50. **Octopuses Collect Shells for Shelter**: Some octopuses gather coconut shells and other objects to create makeshift shelters on the ocean floor, a behavior indicating problem-solving skills and the use of tools.

These intriguing behaviors are vivid examples of how evolution has shaped species to develop unique adaptations for survival, communication, and interaction within their ecosystems.

Delving further into the fascinating behaviors of animals, here are more facts that highlight the extraordinary adaptability and ingenuity found in nature:

51. **Wombats Produce Cube-Shaped Poop**: Wombats have a unique digestive process that shapes their feces into cubes, which they use to mark territory and communicate due to their tendency not to roll away.

52. **Thorn Bugs Mimic Plant Thorns**: Thorn bugs have evolved to look exactly like the thorns on a plant, a form of camouflage that protects them from predators while they feed on plant sap.

53. **Flamingos Bend Their Legs at the Ankle, Not the Knee**: What appears to be the knee is the flamingo's ankle, and their knees are closer to the body, hidden by feathers, helping in their unique wading lifestyle.

54. **Jellyfish Evaporate in the Sun**: Some species of jellyfish are composed of up to 98% water and can evaporate completely when left in the sun for too long, showcasing their unique biological composition.

55. **Male Seahorses Give Birth**: Male seahorses are equipped with a pouch where females deposit eggs. The males then fertilize and carry the eggs until they hatch, a rare example of male pregnancy in the animal kingdom.

56. **Cheetahs Use Their Tails for Steering**: Like a rudder for a boat, a cheetah's tail helps balance and steer while running at high speeds, allowing for sharp turns in pursuit of prey.

57. **Bats Hang Upside Down for Takeoff**: Bats hang upside down so they can easily take off into flight. Their lightweight bodies and strong rear leg muscles are perfectly adapted for this unique launching method.

58. **Giraffe Necks for Heat Regulation**: Beyond reaching high branches, a giraffe's long neck also plays a crucial role in thermoregulation, helping to disperse body heat across its large surface area.

59. **Killer Whales Teach Their Young to Hunt**: Killer whales engage in teaching behaviors, with mothers showing their calves how to hunt using techniques specific to their regional group, indicating cultural transmission of knowledge.

60. **Snails Can Sleep for Years**: Some snail species can enter a hibernation-like state called estivation, lasting up to three years in dry conditions to avoid dehydration, showcasing an extreme survival strategy.

61. **Eagles Lock Talons in a Test of Strength**: Bald eagles perform a dramatic aerial display where they lock talons and spin towards the ground, a behavior used in courtship as well as combat between rivals.

62. **Electric Eels Generate Electricity**: Electric eels can produce electric shocks of up to 600 volts to stun prey or defend themselves, an adaptation achieved through specialized cells called electrolytes.

63. **Penguins Can Drink Salt Water**: Penguins have a gland behind their eyes that filters salt from the water, allowing them to survive without fresh water, a necessary adaptation for their marine lifestyle.

64. **Ants Use Their Bodies to Build Bridges**: Some ant species form bridges with their bodies for others to cross, showcasing remarkable teamwork and problem-solving abilities.

65. **Frogs Use Eyes to Swallow**: Frogs use their eyes to help push food down their throat by retracting them into their heads, a unique mechanism for swallowing.

66. **Parrotfish Sleep in Bubbles**: Parrotfish secrete a mucous cocoon around themselves at night, which masks their scent from predators and serves as a protective barrier.

67. **Sloths Move Slowly to Avoid Detection**: Sloths move at a slow pace to blend in with their surroundings and avoid detection by predators, a survival strategy complemented by their greenish fur that hosts algae.

68. **Moths Navigate by the Moon**: Moths use the moon as a navigation tool, maintaining a constant angular relationship to it, a behavior that sometimes leads them astray with artificial lights.

69. **Camels' Humps Store Fat, Not Water**: A camel's hump is a reservoir of fatty tissue, not water. The fat can be converted to water or energy when food and water are scarce, aiding in their desert survival.

70. **Leafcutter Ants Farm Fungi**: Leafcutter ants cut and collect leaves not for consumption but to cultivate fungus gardens, their primary food source, showcasing an agricultural society among insects.

These examples underscore the complexity and diversity of life on Earth, with each species developing unique strategies to navigate their environments, find food, reproduce, and communica te.

71. **Sharks Can Sense a Heartbeat**: Sharks have special sensory organs called the ampullae of Lorenzini that can detect the electrical fields created by a heartbeat, aiding them in hunting prey.

72. **Owls Can Rotate Their Heads 270 Degrees**: Owls have a unique bone structure and blood vessels that allow them to rotate their heads without cutting off blood supply to the brain, crucial for their hunting technique.

73. **Ducks Have Waterproof Feathers**: Ducks produce oil in a gland near their tails, which they spread over their feathers to make them waterproof, an adaptation essential for their aquatic lifestyle.

74. **Starfish Can Regrow Lost Arms**: Most species of starfish can regrow lost arms, a process that can take months or years, showcasing remarkable regenerative abilities.

75. **Platypuses Glow Under UV Light**: Platypuses have bio-fluorescent fur that glows under ultraviolet light, a feature whose purpose is still not fully understood by scientists.

76. **Porcupines Float in Water**: The air-filled quills of porcupines make them excellent swimmers, and they can use this ability to escape predators.

77. **Coral Reefs Are Made by Living Organisms**: Coral reefs are built by tiny coral polyps that secrete limestone to form a hard shell around their bodies, creating vast underwater structures over thousands of years.

78. **Beavers Create Ecosystems**: By building dams, beavers create new wetland ecosystems, demonstrating nature's ability to engineer environments that support diverse wildlife.

79. **Ravens Can Plan for the Future**: Ravens have been shown to use tools and plan for future events, behaviors that demonstrate cognitive abilities comparable to those of primates.

80. **Squid Can Change Color for Communication**: Squids use chromatophores in their skin to change color and pattern for communication and camouflage, displaying a complex visual language.

81. **Lemurs Use Scent for Communication**: Lemurs have scent glands that they use to mark territory and communicate, an olfactory method of maintaining social hierarchy and signaling reproductive status.

82. **Sea Turtles Navigate Using Earth's Magnetic Field**: Sea turtles use the Earth's magnetic field as a navigational tool to find their way across vast oceans, a phenomenon known as magnetoreception.

83. **Honeyguides Lead Humans to Honey**: The African honeyguide bird can lead humans to bee nests, demonstrating a unique interspecies relationship based on mutual benefit.

84. **Gibbons Sing Duets to Strengthen Bonds**: Gibbon pairs sing complex duets at dawn, a behavior that strengthens their pair bond and marks their territory.

85. **Koalas Have Fingerprints Almost Identical to Humans**: Koalas have fingerprints that are so similar to humans that they can be confused at a crime scene, an evolutionary coincidence.

86. **Birds Use Quantum Mechanics to Navigate**: Some birds, like the European robin, are thought to use quantum mechanics via a process called quantum entanglement in their eyes to navigate during migration.

87. **Chameleons Change Color for Communication, Not Camouflage**: Contrary to popular belief, chameleons primarily change color to communicate their physiological state to other chameleons, rather than for camouflage.

88. **Armadillos Can Carry Leprosy**: Armadillos are one of the few known animals that can carry and transmit leprosy to humans, a curious case of zoonotic disease transmission.

89. **Pigeons Can Recognize Human Faces**: Pigeons can recognize individual human faces and differentiate between them, indicating high visual acuity.

90. **Butterflies Taste With Their Feet**: Butterflies have taste receptors on their feet, allowing them to taste their food by standing on it, an adaptation for identifying suitable plants on which to lay eggs.

91. **Snakes Can See Infrared Radiation**: Some snakes have pits on their faces that can detect infrared radiation, allowing them to see the body heat of their prey even in complete darkness.

92. **Anteaters Don't Have Teeth**: Instead of teeth, anteaters have long, sticky tongues that they use to collect ants and termites, a dietary specialization that influences their physical str ucture.

93. **Mantis Shrimp Have The Most Complex Eyes in the Animal Kingdom**: Their eyes are capable of seeing polarized light and can detect ten times more color than a human, including ultraviolet light.

94. **Wolves Have Different Howls for Different Situations**: Wolves use a variety of howls to communicate everything from location to warnings about predators, demonstrating a complex auditory communication system.

95. **Peacocks Don't Just Display Their Feathers for Mates**: While peacock feather displays are famously used in courtship, they're also employed to intimidate rivals or even to distract preda tor s.

96. **Lobsters Have Blue Blood**: The blue color of lobster blood is due to the presence of hemocyanin, which contains copper, used for oxygen transport in their blood.

97. **Dogs Can Smell Fear**: Dogs are known to pick up on human pheromones that indicate stress or fear, an ability that has likely been honed through thousands of years of domestica tion.

98. **African Elephants Can Communicate Over Long Distances Using Infrasound**: These low-frequency sounds, undetectable to humans, can travel several kilometers, allowing elephants to communicate with each other over long distances.

99. **Bumblebees Can Detect Electric Fields**: Bumblebees can sense the electric field that surrounds a flower, helping them to find nectar, a sense known as electroreception.

100. **Horses Can Read Human Emotions**: Horses have been shown to distinguish between angry and happy human facial expressions, and they react differently to each, indicating a high level of social sensitivity.

These facts further illustrate the depth of wonder the natural world holds, with each species exhibiting behaviors that are both fascinating and vital to their survival.

.

Section 1:2

Astonishing Plant Life

.

The plant kingdom is replete with extraordinary species, each adapted to thrive in its unique environment through remarkable survival mechanisms. Here are 25 fascinating facts about these resilient and innovative organisms:

1. **Venus Flytrap's Rapid Closure**: The Venus flytrap captures insects by rapidly closing its leaves in response to touch stimuli, using a complex mechanism that involves changes in cell pressure.

2. **Baobab Trees Store Water**: Baobab trees can store up to 120,000 liters of water in their trunks to survive the arid conditions of the African savannah.

3. **Sequoias Resist Fire**: The bark of giant sequoias is fire-resistant, which protects the trees from forest fires and allows them to live for thousands of years.

4. **Alpine Plants' UV Reflection**: High-altitude alpine plants have a waxy coating that reflects ultraviolet light, protecting them from intense sun exposure.

5. **Mangroves Filter Salt**: Mangrove trees thrive in saltwater environments by filtering out salt at the root level or excreting it through their leaves.

6. **Corpse Flower Mimics Decay**: The titan arum, or corpse flower, emits a strong odor of decaying flesh to attract pollinators like flies and beetles.

7. **Resurrection Plants Revive from Desiccation**: Resurrection plants can survive extreme dehydration for months or years and revive within hours after receiving water.

8. **Cacti's Nighttime CO2 Storage**: Many cacti open their stomata at night to take in CO_2 (to reduce water loss) and store it for photosynthesis during the day.

9. **Sunflowers Track the Sun**: Young sunflower plants exhibit heliotropism, turning their heads to track the sun from east to west during the day.

10. **Tumbleweeds' Seed Dispersion:** Tumbleweeds detach from their roots and tumble with the wind to spread their seeds over a wider area.

11. **Lotus Effect for Self-Cleaning:** The leaves of the lotus plant have a microscopically bumpy surface that repels water and dirt, a phenomenon known as the lotus effect.

12. **Kelp's Anchor System:** Kelp forests anchor themselves to the ocean floor using a holdfast, a root-like structure, to withstand strong underwater currents.

13. **Pando, The Trembling Giant:** Pando is a clonal colony of quaking aspen in Utah, considered the world's heaviest organism, connected by a single root system.

14. **Cholla Cactus Wooden Skeleton:** The cholla cactus leaves behind a dense wooden skeleton that provides structure and minimizes water loss.

15. **Pitcher Plants' Insect Traps:** Pitcher plants trap insects in a deep cavity filled with digestive liquid, using nectar and color to lure them in.

16. **Arctic Poppy Faces the Sun:** The Arctic poppy grows cup-shaped flowers that track the sun, maximizing solar energy absorption in cold environments.

17. **Rubber Trees' Wound Healing:** When cut, rubber trees release latex, which coagulates and seals wounds to protect against infections and pests.

18. **Creosote Bush's Chemical Warfare:** The creosote bush releases chemicals into the soil to inhibit the growth of competing plant species, a tactic known as allelopathy.

19. **Bamboo's Rapid Growth:** Some species of bamboo can grow up to 91 cm (35 in) within 24 hours, making it one of the fastest-growing plants on Earth.

20. **Welwitschia's Longevity:** The Welwitschia plant, found in the Namib Desert, has only two leaves that grow continuously for up to 1,500 years.

21. **Sundews' Sticky Tentacles:** Sundews capture prey with sticky, glandular tentacles that curl around the insect, enhancing contact with digestive enzymes.

22. **Eelgrass's Underwater Pollination:** Eelgrass is one of the few plants that can pollinate underwater, using the water to disperse pollen.

23. **Saguaro Cactus' Pleated Skin:** The pleated skin of the saguaro cactus allows it to expand and store water during rain, sustaining it through drought periods.

24. **Mosses' Tolerance to Desiccation**: Mosses can survive drying out by entering a dormant state, then rehydrate and resume growth with the return of moisture.

25. **Strangler Figs' Host Takeover**: Strangler figs germinate on other trees and grow roots downward to the ground, eventually enveloping and "strangling" the host tree.

These examples underscore plants' innovative adaptations to their environments, showcasing the incredible diversity and resilience of the plant kingdom.

The botanical world is full of surprises, with plants demonstrating incredible strategies for survival, reproduction, and growth. Here are more fascinating facts about extraordinary plants and their unique mechanisms:

26. **Fireweed Thrives After Fires:** Fireweed is one of the first plants to grow after a forest fire, helping stabilize the soil and prevent erosion while revitalizing the ecosystem.

27. **Hydrangeas Change Color with Soil pH:** The color of hydrangea flowers can change from pink to blue based on the pH level of the soil, which affects the availability of aluminum ions.

28. **Bracken Ferns' Carcinogenic Toxins:** Bracken ferns produce carcinogenic compounds that can be harmful to livestock and humans if ingested in large quantities, a defense mechanism against herbivory.

29. **Dandelion's Seed Parachutes:** Dandelion seeds are equipped with a parachute-like structure that allows them to be carried by the wind, ensuring wide dispersal.

30. **The Giant Water Lily's Supportive Structure**: The giant water lily has a leaf structure that can support significant weight due to its ribbed underside, allowing it to float on water.

31. **Ginkgo Biloba's Resistance to Pollution**: Ginkgo biloba trees are highly resistant to pollution and diseases, making them popular in urban landscaping.

32. **Mustard Plants' Biofumigation:** Some mustard plants can suppress soil-borne pests and diseases through biofumigation, releasing compounds that act as natural fumigants when their tissues are crushed.

33. **Orchids Mimic Their Pollinators**: Many orchids have evolved flowers that mimic the appearance and scent of female insects to attract male pollinators in a deceptive strategy for pollina tion.

34. **Peat Mosses' Water Retention:** Peat mosses can absorb and retain significant amounts of water, up to 20-30 times their dry weight, playing a crucial role in bog ecosystems.

35. **The Sensitive Plant's Rapid Movement:** The sensitive plant (Mimosa pudica) folds its leaves in response to touch, a defense mechanism to deter predators or shading.

36. **Desert Rose's Bulbous Trunk:** The desert rose adapts to arid environments by developing a bulbous trunk for water storage, supporting its survival during droughts.

37. **The Traveler's Tree Stores Water:** The traveler's palm has leaf bases that form cups, collecting and storing rainwater that can be accessed by slicing the base, hence its name.

38. **Ice Plants' Salt Secretion**: Some ice plants can tolerate high salt in soil by excreting excess salt through special glands, which sometimes gives their leaves a frosted appearance.

39. **The Joshua Tree's Moth Pollination:** Joshua trees rely on specific moths for pollination, in a mutualistic relationship where the moth lays its eggs in the flower, and the emerging larvae feed on some of the seeds.

40. **Carnivorous Butterwort's Sticky Leaves:** Butterworts trap small insects on their sticky leaves, digesting them to supplement the poor nutrient availability in their soil.

41. **Coffee Plants' Caffeine as a Pesticide:** The caffeine produced by coffee plants serves as a natural pesticide, deterring herbivores and inhibiting the growth of competing plants.

42. **Bristlecone Pines' Longevity:** Bristlecone pines are among the oldest living organisms on Earth, with some specimens over 5,000 years old, their slow growth and resinous wood contributing to their longevity.

43. **Aloe Vera's Healing Gel**: Aloe vera leaves contain a gel-like substance known for its healing and soothing properties, an adaptation for water storage that also benefits humans.

44. **The Corpse Lily's Massive Bloom:** The corpse lily produces the world's largest single flower, which emits a strong odor of decomposing flesh to attract pollinators like flies.

45. **Rafflesia's Parasitic Lifestyle:** Rafflesia plants are parasites that live inside the vines of their host plants, only emerging to bloom, producing large, meat-colored flowers that emit a foul odor.

46. **Cherry Blossom's Fleeting Blooms:** The short-lived blooms of cherry blossom trees, symbolizing the ephemeral nature of life, are celebrated around the world.

47. **Spider Plants' Air Purification:** Spider plants are known for their ability to purify the air, removing common indoor pollutants and improving indoor air quality.

48. **Witch Hazel's Winter Flowering**: Witch hazel is unique for its ability to flower in the middle of winter, with its fragrant, ribbon-like petals capable of withstanding cold tempera tures.

49. **Cycads' Ancient Lineage.** Cycads are among the oldest groups of seed plants, having survived since the time of the dinosaurs, with little change in their appearance.

50. **The Chocolate Vine's Edible Fruit:** The chocolate vine produces fragrant flowers and edible fruit that, when ripe, have a flavor reminiscent of chocolate, though it's the plant's seed pulp that's consumed.

These facts highlight the incredible diversity and complexity of plant life, exploring the realm of extraordinary plants further reveals a myriad of survival mechanisms, each showcasing the adaptability and ingenuity of plant life across various ecosystems. Here are more fascinating facts about these resilient and innovative organisms:

51. **Night-Blooming Cereus Opens After Dark**: This cactus blooms only at night, with flowers that open after dark and close by morning, adapted to pollination by nocturnal insects and bats.

52. **The Immortal Jellyfish Plant**: Turritopsis dohrnii, often called the "immortal jellyfish," isn't a plant but inspires the naming of a real plant, Selaginella lepidophylla, also known as the "resurrection plant" for its ability to survive almost complete desiccation.

53. **Nepenthes Rajah's Giant Traps**: This pitcher plant produces some of the largest carnivorous traps, capable of holding over 2 liters of water and digesting insects and even small rodents.

54. **Antarctic Hair Grass Thrives in Extreme Cold**: One of the only two vascular plants native to Antarctica has adapted to grow in one of the harshest environments on Earth.

55. **The Living Stones**: Lithops, also known as "living stones," mimic the appearance of stones or pebbles as a form of camouflage from predators.

56. **Arabica Coffee's Wild Origins**: The world's most popular coffee, Arabica, originates from wild plants in the mountains of Ethiopia, showcasing the importance of wild species conservation.

57. **The Great Basin Bristlecone Pine's Wind Sculpting**: Exposed to unrelenting winds, these trees become beautifully sculpted, showcasing nature's artistry alongside their remarkable longevity.

58. **Dragon Blood Trees' Life-Giving Sap:** Native to Socotra, these trees produce a red sap used in traditional medicine and dye, reflecting the deep connection between plants and human culture.

59. **The Sausage Tree's Fruit**: Kigelia africana, or the sausage tree, bears long, sausage-like fruits that are used in traditional medicine and can be hazardous if eaten unprepared.

60. **The 'Suicide Palm' of Madagascar**: Tahina spectabilis flowers once after decades, producing a massive inflorescence before dying, an extraordinary example of semelparity in plants.

61. **Woad Produces Natural Blue Dye:** Historically used to produce a vibrant blue dye, Isatis tinctoria illustrates the varied uses of plants beyond food and medicine.

62. **Ghost Orchids' Ephemeral Beauty**: With no leaves and a seemingly floating flower, the ghost orchid is a rare and mysterious species reliant on a specific fungus for nutrients.

63. **The Screwpine's Aerial Roots**: Pandanus trees, or screwpines, develop stilt-like aerial roots that support them in sandy and unstable soils, showcasing an adaptation to coastal environments.

64. **Cotton Grass Thrives in Bogs:** Eriophorum spp., despite its name, isn't a grass but a sedge that thrives in acidic wetlands, its fluffy, cotton-like seed heads aiding in seed dispersal by wind.

65. **The Bottle Tree's Water Storage:** Baobabs are not the only trees to store water; bottle trees (Brachychiton rupestris) also have a swollen trunk for water storage, adapted to life in arid regions.

66. **Parachute Seeds of the Dandelion**: Going beyond simple wind dispersal, the structure of a dandelion's seed parachute is a marvel of aerodynamics, maximizing dispersal efficiency.

67. **The Flame Lily's Climbing Tendrils**: Gloriosa superba uses tendrils at the tips of its leaves to climb and access sunlight, showcasing an adaptation to forest understories.

68. **Desert Ironwood's Nurse Plant Role**: Serving as a nursery to young plants by providing shade and moisture conservation, the desert ironwood is a keystone species in its ecosystem.

69. **The Wax Plant's Shiny Leaves**: Hoya, known as the wax plant, has thick, shiny leaves adapted to retain moisture, reflecting its origin in tropical and subtropical regions.

70. **The Sea Holly's Metallic Hue**: Eryngium, with its striking blue or metallic-colored bracts, is adapted to attract pollinators while deterring herbivores with its spiny leaves.

71. **Cannonball Tree's Loud Fruit Drop**: Named for its large, spherical fruits that make a loud noise upon hitting the ground, the cannonball tree's method of seed dispersal is as dramatic as it is effective.

72. **Strangler Fig's Lethal Embrace**: Starting life as an epiphyte, the strangler fig eventually envelops its host tree, illustrating a competitive strategy for light and space in dense forests.

73. **Quiver Tree's Thermal Adaptation**: Aloe dichotoma stores water in its trunk and has a reflective surface to combat extreme desert temperatures, serving as a living example of thermal adaptation.

74. **Monkey Puzzle Tree's Prehistoric Origins**: With a name inspired by its intricate, puzzle-like showcasing how plants have evolved a myriad of adaptations to survive and thrive in every environment on Earth.

75. **Rainbow Eucalyptus' Peeling Bark:** The rainbow eucalyptus sheds its bark in patches throughout the year, revealing a bright green layer that gradually matures to give a rainbow effect.

76. **Touch-Me-Not's Explosive Seed Pods**: Mimosa pudica, when touched, folds its leaves defensively, but its seed pods also explode to disperse seeds when ripe, maximizing seed spread.

77. **The New Zealand Christmas Tree**: The pohutukawa tree is known for its vibrant red flowers that bloom around December, contributing to its festive nickname.

78. **African Baobab's Hollow Trunks:** Some baobab trees have large hollow trunks used by animals and humans alike, from shelters to storage, illustrating an unusual symbiosis.

79. **Sand Food's Underground Lifestyle:** Pholisma sonorae, a rare desert plant, lives almost entirely underground, with only its flower emerging above the surface, an adaptation to extreme aridity.

80. **The Corpse Lily's Enormous Size:** Rafflesia arnoldii produces the largest individual flower in the world, but being a parasitic plant, it lacks leaves, stems, and roots, drawing nutrients from its host vine.

81. **Dawn Redwood's Discovery:** Once thought to be extinct and known only from fossils, the dawn redwood was discovered alive in China in the 1940s, a "living fossil" linking past and present.

82. **Amorphophallus Konjac's Stench**: Similar to the corpse flower, this plant emits a foul odor resembling rotting flesh to attract pollinators like flies and beetles.

83. **Victoria Amazonica's Massive Lily Pads**: Capable of supporting significant weight, these giant lily pads showcase a structural design optimized for buoyancy and surface area.

84. **The Honeypot Ant Plant**: Myrmecodia, or ant plants, have evolved a symbiotic relationship with ants, sheltering them in exchange for protection and nutrients from their waste.

85. **Living Fossil' Wollemi Pin**: Known from fossils dating back to the age of dinosaurs, living specimens were found in Australia in the 1990s, offering a direct link to the earth's distant past.

86. **Sea Oats' Dune Formation:** Uniola paniculata plays a crucial role in dune formation and stabilization, with its extensive root system anchoring the sand.

87. **Sundew's Glistening Droplets**: Beyond their carnivorous nature, sundews produce droplets that glisten in the sunlight, attracting unsuspecting prey with their deceptive sparkle.

88. **The Old Man Cactus**: Resembling an elderly gentleman's white hair, the dense white spines of this cactus serve to reflect sunlight, reducing water loss and protecting from the sun.

89. **Persian Silk Tree's Sleepy Leaves**: Also known as the "sleeping tree," its leaves fold up at night or when touched, part of a daily rhythm called nyctinasty.

90. **The Puya Raimondii's Century-Long Life**: Before blooming a single spectacular time and dying, this plant can live for up to a century, growing a towering inflorescence over 9 meters tall.

91. **Welwitschia's Single Pair of Leaves**: Unique to the Namib Desert, this plant grows only two leaves that can reach lengths of up to 8 meters over hundreds of years.

92. **The Christmas Orchid's Seasonal Bloom:** Cattleya percivaliana predictably blooms around Christmas each year, its festive timing giving it its common name.

93. **The Desert Pea's Blood-Red Flowers**: Swainsona formosa, with its striking red petals and black center, is a resilient desert plant, its vivid coloring a warning of its toxicity.

94. **Tillandsia's Air Plant Survival:** Thriving without soil, these plants absorb moisture and nutrients through their leaves from the air, exemplifying extreme adaptability.

95. **The Waterwheel Plant's Underwater Snap Trap**: An aquatic carnivorous plant, it captures prey with rapid underwater snap traps, similar to a submerged Venus flytrap.

96. **Judas Tree's Biblical Legend**: Named for its supposed association with Judas Iscariot, this tree is known for its vibrant pink blooms that appear directly on its branches before the leaves.

97. **The TickleMe Plant's Movements**: Mimosa pudica, when touched, folds its leaves in a defensive mechanism, reacting visibly to touch, heat, or wind.

98. **Moss Ball's Rolling Growth**: Also known as "marimo," these algae balls form in cold lakes with wave action rolling them into spherical shapes, a slow but fascinating growth process.

99. **The Chocolate Cosmos' Scent**: Cosmos atrosanguineus emits a chocolate-like fragrance, a delightful sensory experience not commonly associated with flowers.

100. **The Walking Palm's Migration**: Socratea exorrhiza can "walk" by growing new roots toward the light and letting old ones die, slowly moving the tree over time.

101. **Cycad's Symbiotic Pollination**: Some cycads produce a heat burst to volatilize their scent, attracting specific beetle species for pollination, and showcasing a highly specialized co-evolution.

102. **Silversword's Volcanic Adaptation**: Native to Hawaii, the silversword grows on volcanic soil, its silver leaves reflecting sunlight and conserving moisture, a stunning example of adaptation to extreme conditions.

103. **The Bat Flower's Striking Appearance**: Tacca chantrieri, with its black flowers and long, whisker-like filaments, is one of the most unusual and dramatic flowering plants.

104. **Ocotillo's Leafing After Rain**: Fouquieria splendens rapidly grows leaves after rainfall, losing them during drought, an adaptation to desert living that conserves water.

105. **The Alpine Forget-Me-Not's High Altitude Bloom**: Thriving at elevations up to 12,000 feet, this tiny blue flower demonstrates extreme resilience to cold and UV radiation.

These facts highlight the profound diversity and adaptability of plant life, showcasing a world of botanical wonders that continue to inspire and intrigue scientists, gardeners, and nature enthusiasts alike.

Section 1.3: Mysteries of the Oceans

The deep sea, Earth's final frontier, is home to some of the most bizarre and fascinating creatures known to science. Here are facts about deep-sea discoveries and the unusual marine life forms that inhabit the abyss:

1. **Bioluminescence is Common**: Many deep-sea creatures produce their light through a process called bioluminescence, used for attracting prey, communication, and camouflage.

2. **Giant Squid Eyes**: The giant squid has the largest eyes in the animal kingdom, up to 10 inches in diameter, allowing them to detect light in the profound darkness of the deep sea.

3. **Anglerfish's Deadly Lure**: Female anglerfish possess a luminescent lure that hangs in front of their mouths to attract prey, a characteristic example of the use of bioluminescence.

4. **Hydrothermal Vent Ecosystems**: Discovered in the late 1970s, hydrothermal vents support unique ecosystems that thrive in extreme conditions without sunlight, relying on chemosynthesis rather than photosynthesis.

5. **The Blobfish:** Named the "world's ugliest animal," the blobfish has a gelatinous consistency that allows it to withstand the immense pressure of the deep sea.

6. **Vampire Squid from Hell**: Despite its name, the vampire squid feeds primarily on detritus, using a unique filament to collect particles from the water column.

7. **Yeti Crab's Furry Claws**: Discovered near hydrothermal vents, the yeti crab covers its claws and body in filamentous bacteria, which it may use for detoxifying harmful chemicals or as a food source.

8. **The Black Dragonfish**: Possessing an elongated body and equipped with bioluminescent organs, it can produce a faint red light, invisible to other deep-sea animals, allowing it to hunt undetected.

9. **Zombie Worms**: Also known as bone-eating worms, they feed on the bones of whale carcasses by secreting acid to access the nutrients inside.

10. **Mariana Trench:** The deepest part of the world's oceans, reaching depths of nearly 11 kilometers (about 7 miles), hosts life forms adapted to extreme pressure.

11. **Dumbo Octopus**: Named for its ear-like fins, the Dumbo octopus is one of the deepest-living octopus species, found at depths of up to 7,000 meters.

12. **The Greenland Shark's Longevity**: Greenland sharks are among the longest-living vertebrate species, with some individuals estimated to be over 400 years old.

13. **Barreleye Fish**: This fish has a transparent head and tubular eyes, which can rotate to provide a view directly upwards through its dome, looking for silhouettes of prey above.

14. **Snailfish:** The deepest living fish, the snailfish, has been found at depths of about 8,000 meters, showcasing unique adaptations to survive under extreme pressure.

15. **The Sperm Whale's Deep Dives**: Sperm whales can dive over 2,000 meters deep in search of food, such as the elusive giant squid, staying submerged for up to an hour.

16. **Chemosynthetic Life Forms**: Many deep-sea organisms rely on chemosynthesis, a process that uses chemical reactions to produce energy, instead of sunlight for photosynthesis.

17. **The Mimic Octopus**: Although not exclusively deep-sea, this octopus can imitate the physical likeness and movements of more than fifteen different species, including venomous lionfish, flatfish, and sea snakes.

18. **Deep-Sea Brine Pools**: Underwater lakes of super salty water that can be toxic to most marine life but host unique ecosystems on their edges.

19. **Hydrothermal Vent Octopus**: A species of octopus found living near hydrothermal vents, laying their eggs in warm waters, which may accelerate the hatching process.

20. **Frilled Shark**: Resembling a sea serpent, this deep-sea shark has a wide mouth lined with 25 rows of backward-facing teeth.

21. **The Lanternfish's Light**: Lanternfish are equipped with light-producing organs to help them evade predators and attract prey in pitch-black waters.

22. **Gulper Eel's Giant Mouth**: The gulper eel can unhinge its massive jaw to swallow prey much larger than itself, its stomach can also extend to accommodate its big meals.

23. **The Glass Squid**: This squid's body is almost completely transparent, a natural invisibility cloak to help it evade predators in the deep sea.

24. **Colossal Squid**: Larger than the giant squid, the colossal squid has the largest beak of any squid species and swiveling hooks on the clubs at the ends of its tentacles.

25. **Sea Angels**: Floating through the cold waters, these small, translucent sea slugs flap their wings like angels and are ferocious predators, feeding on the sea butterfly.

The deep ocean continues to be a source of scientific discovery, revealing creatures and phenomena that seem to belong to another world. Here are additional facts about deep-sea discoveries and the peculiar life forms dwelling in the abyss:

26. **Transparent Anemone**: Found on the ocean floor, this creature uses its transparency as a form of camouflage, making it nearly invisible to predators and prey alike.

27. **Comb Jellies' Light Show**: Comb jellies, or ctenophores, use rows of cilia to propel through the water, refracting light into dazzling rainbow patterns.

28. **Deep-Sea Coral Gardens**: Unlike their sunlit, shallow-water counterparts, deep-sea corals do not rely on photosynthesis and often grow in complete darkness, forming intricate and biodiverse ha bita ts.

29. **The Ice Worm**: Discovered in polar ice and cold seafloors, ice worms thrive in temperatures that freeze most life, breaking down complex carbohydrates in the ice.

30. **Psychrolutes marcidus**: Commonly known as the "smooth-head blobfish," it's adapted to the extreme pressure of the deep sea with a density slightly less than water, allowing it to float above the seafloor.

31. **The Osedax Worm**: Also known as the "whale bone-eating worm," it has a unique ability to bore into and digest whale bones on the deep-sea floor, obtaining sustenance from the lipids.

32. **Deep-Sea Hatchetfish**: Named for its distinctively thin, flat body resembling a hatchet's blade, this fish uses bioluminescence for counter-illumination, blending with the light from above to avoid preda tor s.

33. **Giant Isopods**: These deep-sea relatives of woodlice can grow to be over a foot long, resembling giant pill bugs, adapted to scavenging the deep ocean's floor for food.

34. **The Telescope Octopus**: Known for its transparent, elongated body and barrel-shaped eyes, the telescope octopus can rotate its eyes to scan its surroundings, a rare trait among octopuses.

35. **Ping-Pong Tree Sponge**: This carnivorous sponge, with its ball-shaped appendages on branching limbs, captures small creatures that come into contact with its sticky surface.

36. **Predatory Tunicates**: Also known as "sea squirts," these sessile creatures filter feed most of their life but some deep-sea species are known to actively capture and consume prey by enveloping them.

37. **The Goblin Shark**: With a distinctive elongated snout and protruding jaw, the goblin shark can thrust its jaw forward at high speed to catch prey, a startling adaptation to deep-sea hunting.

38. **Brachiopods**: These ancient creatures, resembling clams but with a different internal structure, have existed for over 500 million years and can be found in the deep sea, living in cold, nutrient-rich waters.

39. **Deep-Sea Vents' Tube Worms**: Thriving in extreme conditions without sunlight, these worms rely on symbiotic bacteria within their bodies to convert thermal vent chemicals into organic matter.

40. **The Deep-Sea Dragonfish**: With large, fang-like teeth and a bioluminescent lure, the dragonfish is a formidable predator, capable of producing a faint, eerie glow to attract its prey.

41. **Chimaeras or Ghost Sharks**: Ancient relatives of sharks and rays, these deep-sea fish have soft bodies and elongated, wing-like pectoral fins, giving them a ghostly appearance.

42. **The Midnight Zone's Life**: Beyond 1,000 meters, in the bathypelagic zone or the "midnight zone," light does not penetrate, and creatures must survive in perpetual darkness.

43. **Giant Sea Spiders**: These arthropods, found in various sizes, have extremely long legs compared to their body size and can grow larger in the cold, high-pressure conditions of the deep sea.

44. **The Moa Moa**: Also known as the sunfish, it dives to deep depths to feed, despite its ungainly appearance, and is known for its large size and peculiar shape.

45. **Deep-Sea Loriciferans**: Discovered to be the first multicellular organisms capable of an anaerobic existence, these tiny creatures can live without oxygen, a breakthrough in understanding life in hypoxic conditions.

46. **The Atolla Jellyfish**: Also known as the "alarm jelly," it emits a series of bioluminescent flashes when attacked, possibly to attract a larger predator to its attacker.

47. **Casper Octopus**: Discovered near the Hawaiian Islands, this almost completely transparent octopus has a ghost-like appearance, showcasing the variety of camouflage strategies in the deep sea.

48. **The Scaly-Foot Gastropod**: Found near hydrothermal vents, this snail has a unique iron-clad shell and scales, offering protection from predators and the harsh environment.

49. **Deep-Sea Red Jellyfish**: With a translucent red dome and long trailing tentacles, this jellyfish uses its coloration as camouflage in the deep, where red light does not penetrate.

50. **The Narcomedusae**: A group of deep-sea jellyfish known for their unusual reproductive strategy; mothers carry their young on their tentacles until they are ready to fend for themselves.

The unexplored depths of our oceans hold mysteries and species that defy imagination. Here's a continuation of the intriguing discoveries and peculiar life forms dwelling in the abyss:

51. **The Sea Toad**: An anglerfish that walks on the seabed with its fin that has evolved into leg-like structures, showcasing a remarkable adaptation to its environment.

52. **Barophiles or Piezophiles**: Microorganisms that not only survive but thrive under extreme pressure in the deep sea, offering insights into the limits of life on Earth and possibly other planets.

53. **The Venus Flytrap Anemone**: Resembling the terrestrial plant, this deep-sea anemone snaps shut on prey that ventures too close, illustrating convergent evolution in hunting strategies.

54. **The Deep-sea Cucumber**: Found in the abyssal plains, these creatures ingest sediment, extracting nutrients and playing a crucial role in the deep-sea ecosystem's nutrient cycle.

55. **Glowing Siphonophores**: These colonial organisms, related to jellyfish, form long, bioluminescent chains in the deep sea to lure and capture prey with their stinging cells.

56. **The Megamouth Shark**: A rare deep-sea shark species discovered in 1976, known for its enormous mouth, used for filter-feeding plankton.

57. **Luminous Lanternsharks**: Small sharks that emit light from their bodies, possibly for camouflage, communication, and attracting prey or mates in the pitch-black depths.

58. **The Cookiecutter Shark**: Named for its circular bite marks on prey, this small shark attaches to larger marine animals, removing cookie-shaped plugs of flesh.

59. **Deep-sea Brachiopods**: Unlike their shallow-water relatives, these ancient creatures thrive in deep, cold waters, resembling clams but with a completely different internal anatomy.

60. **The Frilled Shark**: With a body resembling an eel and a prehistoric lineage, this shark species captures its prey with a sudden, snake-like lunge.

61. **Ctenophores without Tentacles**: Unlike their surface relatives, some deep-sea comb jellies lack tentacles, opening their mouths wide to engulf prey whole.

62. **The Christmas Tree Worm**: Found on coral reefs rather than the deep sea, its spiraling, tree-like appendages are used for both feeding and respiration.

63. **The Hydrothermal Vent Snail**: Coated with iron sulfide armor, these snails are adapted to one of the most extreme environments on Earth, near hydrothermal vents.

64. **The Deep-sea Hatchetfish's Camouflage**: Its silvery body reflects the faint light from above, making it nearly invisible to predators looking upward.

65. **Sea Pens**: Resembling quill pens, these colonial organisms are named for their shape and are found on the ocean floor, housing numerous polyps that feed on passing particles.

66. **The Glass Octopus**: Almost completely transparent, this elusive octopus avoids predation through its near-invisibility, with only its digestive system, eyes, and the optic nerve visible.

67. **Amphipods in Dragon Scale**: Discovered in deep-sea hydrothermal vent fields, these tiny creatures are covered in what looks like dragon scales, possibly as protection against the extreme environment.

68. **The Deep-sea "Elvis Worm**: Named for its iridescent, sequin-like scales that reminded scientists of Elvis Presley's jumpsuits, this polychaete worm adds a touch of glamour to the ocean depths.

69. **The Phantom Jellyfish**: With its delicate, umbrella-like bell and long, trailing tentacles, this ghostly jellyfish drifts in the deep sea, preying on small fish and other jellies.

70. **The Benthic Siphonophore**: Unlike its floating relatives, this species lives on the seafloor,

spreading its tentacles to catch passing prey, a unique adaptation among siphonophores.

71. **The Predatory Tunicate**: Anchored to the seafloor, these sessile creatures resemble a venus flytrap, snapping shut on unsuspecting prey that drifts into their open cavity.

72. **Gigantism in Isopods**: The phenomenon of deep-sea gigantism is exemplified by the giant isopods, related to terrestrial pillbugs but can grow to the size of a football.

73. **The Kiwa Crab**: Also known as the "yeti crab" for its hairy claws and arms, it cultivates bacteria on its fur, which it may eat, a unique example of farming in the animal kingdom.

74. **The Deep-Sea Skate**: These relatives of rays and sharks use hydrothermal vents to incubate their egg cases, a behavior akin to using a natural underwater incubator.

75. **The Dumbo Octopus' Flapping Fins**: Resembling the ears of Disney's Dumbo, these fins help the octopus to hover and maneuver through the water, a gentle giant of the deep sea.

The deep sea remains one of the least explored and understood ecosystems on our planet, teeming with life forms that challenge our perceptions. Here are additional intriguing facts about the discoveries and marine life found in these hidden depths.

76. **The Silky Shark's Deep Dives**: Known for its sleek, smooth skin, the silky shark undertakes deep dives into the abyss to hunt, demonstrating a remarkable adaptation to varying oceanic pressures.

77. **Giant Tube Worms**: These worms thrive near hydrothermal vents, forming symbiotic relationships with bacteria that convert vent chemicals into organic compounds, enabling the worms to survive without sunlight.

78. **The Midnight Zone's Ecosystem**: Beyond 1,000 meters, in the bathypelagic zone, life exists in complete darkness, relying on marine snow (organic material falling from upper layers) for sustenance.

79. **The Deep-Sea Lizardfish**: A fierce predator, this fish has a mouth full of sharp teeth, including extra ones on its tongue, designed to grasp slippery prey in the darkness.

80. **The Pompeii Worm**: One of the most heat-tolerant terrestrial animals known, it lives on hydrothermal vents, with bacteria in its fleece-like fibers possibly protecting it from heat and toxic c hemica ls.

81. **Deep-Sea Red Devils**: Squids in the abyssal zone, like the Dana octopus squid, use bioluminescence to startle predators and lure prey, showcasing the diverse use of light in the deep ocean.

82. **The Sea Spider's Peculiar Feeding**: Using a proboscis to suck nutrients from soft-bodied invertebrates, these arthropods challenge our traditional views of spider feeding habits.

83. **Sperm Whale vs. Giant Squid Battles**: Evidence of epic battles between sperm whales and giant squids comes from scars found on whales and squid beaks discovered in whale stomachs, highlighting the dramatic predator-prey relationships in the deep.

84. **Bioluminescent Octopuses**: Some deep-sea octopuses, like the Stauroteuthis synthesis, emit light from suckers on their arms, which might help in attracting prey or communicating.

85. **The Patagonian Toothfish**: Living in cold, deep waters, this fish has antifreeze proteins in its blood to prevent ice crystals from forming, showcasing an extreme adaptation to cold environments.

86. **The Deep-Sea "Mushroom**: Discovered relatively recently, these enigmatic organisms challenge our understanding of the tree of life, with some not fitting into existing categories of plant, animal, or fungi.

87. **Giant Oarfish**: Often mistaken for sea serpents, these elongated fish can reach lengths of over 8 meters and are believed to inhabit deep waters, though they are rarely seen.

88. **The Lanternfish's Diurnal Migration**: Lanternfish undertake the largest daily migration of any animal, moving vertically through the water column to feed at night and hide in the deep during the day.

89. **The Football Fish's Luminous Lure**: Part of the anglerfish family, this deep-sea predator uses a bioluminescent appendage to attract prey in pitch-black waters.

90. **Deep-Sea Nudibranchs**: Known for their bright colors and intricate shapes in shallow waters, some species of nudibranchs thrive in deep-sea environments, feeding on sponges and other inver tebra tes.

91. **The Walrus's Deep Dives**: While not exclusively a deep-sea animal, walruses can dive to depths of 100 meters in search of benthic bivalves, showcasing remarkable adaptability.

92. **Viperfish's Hinged Jaw**: With teeth too large to fit inside its mouth, the viperfish's jaw is hinged, allowing it to engulf prey almost as big as itself in the deep sea.

93. **The Deep-Sea Holothurian**: These sea cucumbers ingest sediments, extracting nutrients and playing a vital role in recycling organic matter on the ocean floor.

94. **Barreleye Fish with Transparent Head**: This fish has a completely transparent head, with barrel- shaped eyes inside that can look upward through its skull to spot prey above.

95. **Snipe Eels' Unique Jaws**: Snipe eels have unusually elongated jaws, enabling them to feed on small crustaceans and fish in the deep sea, a specialization for feeding in the abyss.

96. **The Greenland Shark's Slow Lifestyle**: With a diet that includes polar bears and reindeer remains, this cold-water shark exhibits a slow, scavenging lifestyle, living in deep, icy waters.

97. **Challenger Deep Benthos**: The deepest known point in the Earth's seabed, Challenger Deep hosts life despite the extreme pressure, including amphipods and other resilient species.

98. **The Coelacanth**: Once thought extinct and known only from fossils, the coelacanth was rediscovered in deep waters, providing insights into the transition of life from sea to land.

99. **Hydrozoans in the Deep**: Deep-sea hydrozoans, related to jellyfish, form intricate colonies that can resemble fans, trees, or feathers, playing a role in the deep-sea food web.

100. **The Abyssal Sea Cucumber**: Inhabiting depths beyond 4,000 meters, these cucumbers are essential detritivores, processing sediments and recycling nutrients in the deep-sea ecosystem.

These additional facts further illuminate the extraordinary adaptations and life forms thriving in the deep sea, underscoring the vastness and complexity of life in the Earth's largest habitat.

Chapter 2: Phenomenal Human Achievements

Section 2.1: Architectural Marvels

The world's most iconic buildings and structures aren't just feats of architecture and engineering; they are symbols of human aspiration, culture, and history. Here are 25 fascinating stories behind some of these monumental creations:

1. **The Eiffel Tower (Paris, France)**: Originally a temporary exhibit for the 1889 World's Fair, the Eiffel Tower was almost dismantled in 1909 but was saved because it served as a valuable radiotelegraph station.

2. **The Great Wall of China**: Stretching over 21,000 kilometers, it's a collection of walls built at different times by various dynasties, primarily as a defense against invasions from the north.

3. **The Colosseum (Rome, Italy):** Constructed from AD 70-80, the Colosseum could hold 50,000 spectators, showcasing ancient Rome's engineering prowess and its social and political life.

4. **Taj Mahal (Agra, India):** A symbol of love, this marble mausoleum was built by Emperor Shah Jahan in memory of his wife Mumtaz Mahal, who died during childbirth in 1631.

5. **Machu Picchu (Peru):** This 15th-century Inca citadel was abandoned a century later, possibly due to smallpox, and remained unknown to the outside world until 1911 when it was rediscovered by Hiram Bingham.

6. **Petra (Jordan):** Known as the "Rose City" for the color of the stone from which it is carved, Petra was the capital of the Nabatean Kingdom in the 4th century BC and is famous for its rock-cut architecture and water conduit system.

7. **Sydney Opera House (Australia):** Its design was selected through an international competition, and its construction was so complex that it ended up costing 14 times the original estimate and was completed 10 years later, in 1973.

8. **The Statue of Liberty (New York, USA):** A gift from France to the United States in 1886, it was a symbol of freedom and democracy, designed by Frédéric Auguste Bartholdi and built by Gustave Eiffel.

9. **The Leaning Tower of Pisa (Italy):** Construction began in the 12th century, but the tower began to lean during construction due to soft ground on one side, which was unable to support the structure's weight.

10. **The Parthenon (Athens, Greece):** Completed in 432 BC, this temple dedicated to the goddess Athena is considered a masterpiece of Doric architecture and symbolizes the glory of ancient Greece.

11. **The Burj Khalifa (Dubai, UAE):** Standing at 828 meters, it's the world's tallest building since 2010, designed to symbolize Dubai's urban transformation and to gain international recognition.

12. **The Sagrada Familia (Barcelona, Spain):** Begun in 1882 and still under construction, this basilica combines Gothic and Art Nouveau forms, reflecting architect Antoni Gaudí's innovative vision and devout spirituality.

13. **Stonehenge (Wiltshire, England):** A prehistoric monument dating back to 3000 BC, its circle of standing stones remains a mystery, with theories about its purpose ranging from an astronomical observatory to a religious site.

14. **The Forbidden City (Beijing, China):** For over 500 years, this palace complex served as the home of emperors and their households, as well as the ceremonial and political center of the Chinese government.

15. **The Empire State Building (New York, USA):** Once the world's tallest building, it was constructed in just over a year during the Great Depression, symbolizing American resilience and ambition.

16. **Christ the Redeemer (Rio de Janeiro, Brazil):** This art deco statue of Jesus Christ, completed in 1931, overlooks Rio from the Corcovado mountain, symbolizing peace and redemption.

17. **The Kremlin (Moscow, Russia):** A historic fortified complex at the heart of Moscow, it has been the official residence of the President of the Russian Federation and serves as a symbol of Russian statehood.

18. **The Lotus Temple (New Delhi, India**): Completed in 1986, this Bahá'í House of Worship is notable for its flowerlike shape, promoting unity and inviting worshipers of all faiths.

19. **St. Basil's Cathedral (Moscow, Russia):** Famous for its colorful, onion-shaped domes, it was commissioned by Ivan the Terrible in the 16th century and stands as a cultural symbol of Russia.

20. **Neuschwanstein Castle (Bavaria, Germany):** Commissioned by Ludwig II of Bavaria as a retreat and homage to Richard Wagner, the castle is known for its fairy-tale look and inspired Disneyland's Sleeping Beauty Castle.

21. **The Pantheon (Rome, Italy):** Almost two thousand years after it was built, the Pantheon dome is still the world's largest unreinforced concrete dome, originally a temple to all the gods of Ancient Rome.

22. **Alhambra (Granada, Spain):** A stunning example of Muslim art in Europe, this fortress and palace complex epitomizes the Moorish culture in Southern Spain and its historical interaction with Christian rulers.

23. **The Shard (London, UK):** Renzo Piano's skyscraper, completed in 2012, is Europe's tallest, designed to resemble a shard of glass and symbolize London's futuristic aspirations.

24. **The Giza Pyramids (Egypt):** One of the Seven Wonders of the Ancient World, these tombs built for pharaohs showcase the ancient Egyptians' architectural innovation and understanding of ma thema tics.

25. **Fallingwater (Pennsylvania, USA):** Designed by Frank Lloyd Wright in 1935, this house over a waterfall is a masterpiece of organic architecture, blending harmoniously with its natural sur roundings.

Each of these iconic structures tells a unique story of cultural identity, technological advancement, and human endeavor, reflecting the diversity and creativity of civilizations around the world.

26. **The Chrysler Building (New York, USA):** Emblematic of the Art Deco era, it was the world's tallest building upon completion in 1930, known for its terraced crown and steel spire.

27. **The White House (Washington D.C., USA):** The official residence and workplace of the U.S. President since John Adams in 1800, its design was selected through a competition won by James Hoban.

28. **Hagia Sophia (Istanbul, Turkey):** A masterpiece of Byzantine architecture, it served as a cathedral, mosque, and now a museum, symbolizing the city's diverse religious history.

29. **Notre-Dame Cathedral (Paris, France):** This medieval cathedral is a pinnacle of French Gothic architecture, renowned for its size, antiquity, and the relics it houses, including the Crown of Thorns.

30. **The Space Needle (Seattle, USA):** Built for the 1962 World's Fair, its futuristic design symbolized humanity's Space Age aspirations, featuring a revolving restaurant and observation deck.

31. **Mount Rushmore (South Dakota, USA):** Carved into the granite face of Mount Rushmore are the 60-foot heads of Presidents Washington, Jefferson, Lincoln, and Roosevelt, representing the first 150 years of American history.

32. **The Hoover Dam (Nevada/Arizona, USA):** Constructed during the Great Depression, it's an engineering marvel that provided jobs, water storage, flood control, and hydroelectric power.

33. **The Golden Gate Bridge (San Francisco, USA):** An engineering marvel and one of the most internationally recognized symbols of the United States, it was the longest and tallest suspension bridge in the world at its completion in 1937.

34. **The Louvre (Paris, France):** Originally a royal palace, the Louvre was transformed into a public museum during the French Revolution and is now home to tens of thousands of works of art, including the Mona Lisa.

35. **The Tower of London (London, UK):** A historic castle on the north bank of the River Thames, it has served as a royal palace, prison, armory, and treasury, and houses the Crown Jewels of England.

36. **Westminster Abbey (London, UK**): An architectural masterpiece of the 13th to 16th centuries, this Gothic abbey is the coronation and burial site of British monarchs.

37. **The Kremlin and Red Square (Moscow, Russia):** The heart of Russian political power and the site of historic coronations, parades, and funerals, Red Square is dominated by the colorful domes of St. Basil's Cathedral and the walls of the Kremlin.

38. **The Shard (London, UK):** Standing as a symbol of modern London, The Shard was designed by Renzo Piano to resemble a shard of glass and is the tallest building in the UK.

39. **The Willis Tower (Chicago, USA):** Known as the Sears Tower until 2009, it was the tallest building in the world when completed in 1973 and is known for its innovative design that includes nine framed tubes.

40. **The Guggenheim Museum (Bilbao, Spain):** Designed by Frank Gehry, this museum is famed for its revolutionary architecture and revitalization of the Bilbao cityscape.

41. **The CN Tower (Toronto, Canada):** Once the world's tallest free-standing structure, it symbolizes Toronto's skyward expansion and Canada's technological advancement.

42. **Petronas Twin Towers (Kuala Lumpur, Malaysia):** The world's tallest twin towers, they symbolize Malaysia's ambitions and are known for the sky bridge connecting the two buildings.

43. **The Dome of the Rock (Jerusalem):** An Islamic shrine located on the Temple Mount, it is one of the oldest and most recognizable Islamic structures in the world.

44. **The Great Pyramid of Giza (Egypt):** The oldest of the Seven Wonders of the Ancient World and the only one to remain largely intact, it represents a monumental achievement in Egyptian architecture.

45. **Angkor Wat (Cambodia):** Originally constructed as a Hindu temple, it was transformed into a Buddhist temple by the end of the 12th century and is admired for its grand scale and intricate car vings.

46. **The Lincoln Memorial (Washington D.C., USA):** Dedicated to President Abraham Lincoln, this symbol of American freedom attracts millions of visitors who come to reflect on Lincoln's legacy and the civil rights movement.

47. **The Capitol Building (Washington D.C., USA):** Home of the United States Congress and the seat of the legislative branch of the U.S. federal government, its iconic dome is a symbol of democracy.

48. **The Pantheon (Rome, Italy):** Among the best-preserved of all Ancient Roman buildings, it has been in continuous use throughout its history and is known for its large dome and oculus.

49. **The Sydney Harbour Bridge (Australia):** Nicknamed "The Coathanger" because of its arch-based design, this bridge was the world's widest long-span bridge at the time of its construction in 1932.

50. **The Berlin Wall (Berlin, Germany):** Constructed by the German Democratic Republic in 1961, its fall in 1989 became a powerful symbol of the end of the Cold War and the triumph of freedom.

51. **The Atomium (Brussels, Belgium):** Built for the 1958 Brussels World's Fair (Expo 58), it represents an iron crystal magnified 165 billion times, symbolizing peace through scientific progress.

52. **Museu Oscar Niemeyer (Curitiba, Brazil):** Known as the "Eye Museum" for its eye-shaped design, it reflects Niemeyer's vision of architecture as a form of art and a means to evoke human emotion and creativity.

53. **Burj Al Arab (Dubai, UAE):** Often described as the world's only 7-star hotel, its sail-shaped structure has become an iconic symbol of Dubai's luxury and opulence.

54. **The Gateway Arch (St. Louis, USA):** Symbolizing the westward expansion of the United States, its catenary curve shape is a feat of modern engineering.

55. **Las Lajas Sanctuary (Colombia):** Built inside the canyon of the Guáitara River, this Gothic revival church is a pilgrimage site and a testament to Colombian engineering and devotion.

56. **The Shard (London, UK):** Renzo Piano's skyscraper, the tallest building in Western Europe when completed, symbolizes the city's ambition and has reshaped London's skyline.

57. **Himeji Castle (Japan):** Known as "White Heron Castle" for its elegant, white appearance, it is considered the finest surviving example of prototypical Japanese castle architecture.

58. **The Flatiron Building (New York, USA):** One of the city's first skyscrapers, its unique triangular shape was designed to fit the narrow plot of land at the intersection of Fifth Avenue and Broadway.

59. **The Royal Pavilion (Brighton, UK):** An exotic palace built as a seaside retreat

for King George IV, its Indian and Chinese architectural elements reflect the British Empire's reach and the king's eccentric taste.

60. **The Alhambra (Granada, Spain**): This fortress-palace complex is a stunning example of Moorish architecture, showcasing intricate Islamic art and landscaped gardens, reflecting the cultural heritage of the Nasrid dynasty.

61. **The Basilica of Sacré-Cœur (Paris, France):** Situated at the city's highest point on Montmartre, its white domes are a symbol of penance, built in memory of the French victims of the Franco-Prussian War.

62. **The Cathedral of Brasília (Brasília, Brazil):** Designed by Oscar Niemeyer, its hyperboloid structure is composed of 16 concrete columns, representing two hands moving upwards to heaven.

63. **The High Line (New York, USA):** A former New York Central Railroad spur transformed into an elevated greenway, it has inspired cities worldwide to repurpose disused infrastructure into public spaces.

64. **The Shard (London, UK):** This skyscraper symbolizes London's financial prosperity and architectural ambition, transforming the skyline with its distinctive, shard-like design.

65. **The Belem Tower (Lisbon, Portugal):** A fortified tower built in the early 16th century to guard the entrance to Lisbon's harbor, it's a monument to the Age of Discoveries and Portugal's maritime expansions.

66. **Rialto Bridge (Venice, Italy):** One of the oldest bridges spanning the Grand Canal, its current iteration was completed in 1591, showcasing Venice's architectural and engineering prowess.

67. **The Blue Mosque (Istanbul, Turkey**): Famous for its blue tiles adorning the interior walls, it was built during the rule of Ahmed I to reassert Ottoman power.

68. **The Gherkin (London, UK):** Officially known as 30 St Mary Axe, its unique shape and energy-efficient design have made it an icon of modern London.

69. **The United States Capitol (Washington D.C., USA):** The meeting place of the United States Congress and one of the most symbolically important and architecturally impressive buildings in the nation.

70. **The Transamerica Pyramid (San Francisco, USA):** Once the tallest building in San Francisco, its pyramid shape was designed to allow more light and air on the streets below.

71. **La Sagrada Familia (Barcelona, Spain):** Beyond Gaudí's architectural masterpiece, this basilica incorporates Christian symbolism and elements of naturalistic design, aiming to connect the divine and the earthly.

72. **The Brooklyn Bridge (New York, USA):** Completed in 1883, it was the first steel-wire suspension bridge, symbolizing New York's technological innovation and growth.

73. **The Burj Al Arab (Dubai, UAE):** Its sail-like silhouette on the Dubai coastline was designed to reflect the city's maritime heritage and luxurious modern identity.

74. **St. Paul's Cathedral (London, UK):** Sir Christopher Wren's masterpiece survived the Blitz of WWII, becoming a symbol of hope and resilience to Londoners and the British people.

75. **The Pompidou Center (Paris, France):** With its high-tech architecture, exposing its structural and functional systems, it challenged traditional museum concepts and revitalized the Beaubourg area.

76. **Jantar Mantar (Jaipur, India):** An astronomical observation site that reflects the scientific and architectural genius of Maharaja Sawai Jai Singh II in the early 18th century.

77. **Casa Milà (Barcelona, Spain):** Also known as La Pedrera, this modernist building by Antoni Gaudí features a self-supporting stone facade and revolutionary structural innovations.

78. **Forth Bridge (Scotland, UK):** A symbol of Scottish engineering and innovation, this cantilever railway bridge was the longest in the world when it opened in 1890.

79. **The Lotus Temple (New Delhi, India):** Resembling a lotus flower, this Bahá'í House of Worship is notable for its open design, inviting worshipers of all faiths.

80. **The Hoover Dam (Nevada/Arizona, USA):** An engineering marvel of the 20th century, it provided much-needed water and hydroelectric power to the American Southwest during the Great Depression.

81. **The Winter Palace (St. Petersburg, Russia):** Once the official residence of the Russian monarchs, it now houses the Hermitage Museum, one of the largest and oldest museums in the world.

82. **The Tokyo Tower (Tokyo, Japan):** Inspired by the Eiffel Tower, it functions as a communication and observation tower, becoming a symbol of Japan's post-war rebirth as a major economic power.

83. **The Rock of Gibraltar (Gibraltar):** Strategically important, this limestone monolith at the southern tip of the Iberian Peninsula has been a symbol of strength and resilience throughout history.

84. **The Kaaba (Mecca, Saudi Arabia):** The most sacred site in Islam, Muslims around the world face the Kaaba during their daily prayers, symbolizing unity and direction in faith.

85. **The Willis (Sears) Tower (Chicago, USA):** Its innovative design using bundled tubes not only made it the world's tallest building at its completion but also set new standards for skyscraper design.

86. **The Great Sphinx of Giza (Egypt):** With the body of a lion and the head of a human, it's one of the world's oldest and largest monolith statues, still shrouded in mystery regarding its original purpose and construction.

87. **The Hollywood Sign (Los Angeles, USA):** Originally an advertisement for a local real estate development, it has become a symbol of the entertainment industry and dreams of fame.

88. **The Shard (London, UK):** As Western Europe's tallest building, it embodies the financial ascent and panoramic ambition of London's skyline, offering sweeping views of the capital.

89. **Christ the Redeemer (Rio de Janeiro, Brazil):** This towering statue of Jesus Christ atop Mount Corcovado is not only a symbol of Brazilian Christianity but also offers panoramic views of Rio.

90. **Mount Rushmore (South Dakota, USA):** Carved into the granite face of Mount Rushmore are the heads of four U.S. presidents, symbolizing the nation's birth, growth, development, and preservation.

91. **The Space Needle (Seattle, USA):** An icon of the Pacific Northwest, it was built for the 1962 World's Fair and has since symbolized innovation and the spirit of the region.

92. **The Acropolis (Athens, Greece):** This ancient citadel contains the remains of several ancient buildings of great architectural and historical significance, the most famous being the Parthenon.

93. **The Hagia Sophia (Istanbul, Turkey):** A centerpiece of religious life in Istanbul for over 1,500 years, it has served as a cathedral, mosque, and now a museum, symbolizing the city's complex history.

94. **The Gherkin (London, UK):** Officially 30 St Mary Axe, its unique design not only defines London's skyline but also represents the city's modern architectural ambitions.

95. Originally constructed as a **Hindu temple** dedicated to the god Vishnu, it was transformed into a Buddhist temple by the end of the 12th century. Angkor Wat is a symbol of Cambodia's heart and soul, a masterpiece of Khmer architecture renowned for its grand scale and intricate artistry.

96. **The Great Mosque of Córdoba (Spain):** Now a cathedral, its origins as a mosque are evident in the striking striped arches and expansive prayer hall. It stands as a testament to the religious and cultural exchanges that have shaped Spain, reflecting the historical Islamic influence in Andalusia.

97. **The CN Tower (Toronto, Canada):** Once the world's tallest freestanding structure, the CN Tower symbolizes Toronto's skyward aspirations and Canada's technological achievements. Its construction in 1976 marked a milestone in engineering, offering panoramic views and broadcasting capabilities.

98. **The Pyramids of Giza (Egypt):** The only surviving ancient wonder, the pyramids are monumental tombs built for Egypt's Pharaohs. Their precise alignment with the stars and massive scale reflects the ancient Egyptians' architectural skill and their beliefs in the afterlife.

99. **The International Space Station (Orbiting Earth):** Though not a building on Earth, the ISS represents what humanity can achieve in terms of international cooperation and space habitation. Orbiting the planet, it's a symbol of scientific advancement, exploration, and the potential for future space colonization.

100. **The Shard (London, UK):** Renzo Piano's innovative design for The Shard incorporates glass facets that reflect sunlight and the sky above, changing its appearance according to the weather and time of day. As the tallest building in the UK, it marks a point of convergence for business, tourism, and high-altitude dining in London, further cementing the city's status as a global capital.

These structures, spanning from ancient times to the modern day, embody the diversity of human creativity and our relentless pursuit of advancement, be it in the realms of spirituality, defense, living, or exploration.

Section 2.2: Record-Breaking Feats

Human achievements across sports, science, and endurance showcase the incredible limits to which people can push themselves. Here are 25 extraordinary human records that highlight these feats:

1. **Fastest 100m Sprint:** Usain Bolt of Jamaica set the men's world record for the 100m sprint at 9.58 seconds during the World Athletics Championships in 2009 in Berlin, showcasing unparalleled speed.

2. **Deepest Solo Submarine Dive**: In 2019, Victor Vescovo descended 10,928 meters (35,853 feet) into the Mariana Trench, the deepest point of the world's oceans, setting the record for the deepest solo submarine dive.

3. **Most Nobel Prizes:** The United States leads the world with the most Nobel Prize winners, showcasing the country's enduring influence and contributions to science, literature, and peace.

4. **Longest Time in Space**: Russian cosmonaut Gennady Padalka holds the record for the most cumulative time spent in space, amassing a total of 878 days over five missions.

5. **Highest Free Solo Climb**: Alex Honnold ascended El Capitan in Yosemite National Park without ropes or safety gear in 2017, a feat documented in the film "Free Solo," showcasing extreme physical and mental endurance.

6. **Fastest Marathon**: Eliud Kipchoge of Kenya set the men's world record for the fastest marathon time at 2 hours, 1 minute, and 39 seconds during the Berlin Marathon in 2018.

7. **Longest Human Lifespan**: Jeanne Calment of France lived to be 122 years and 164 days old, the longest confirmed human lifespan in history, passing away in 1997.

8. **First Person to Reach Space**: Yuri Gagarin, a Soviet cosmonaut, became the first human to journey into outer space and complete an orbit of the Earth on April 12, 1961.

9. **Heaviest Aircraft Lifted**: In 1987, Ukrainian strongman Paul Anderson lifted the back part of a plane weighing 6,270 kg (13,840 lbs), setting a record for the heaviest aircraft ever lifted by a human.

10. **Fastest Circumnavigation by Bicycle (Men):** Mark Beaumont of the UK set the record for cycling around the world in 78 days, 14 hours, and 40 minutes in 2017, covering 18,032 miles across 16 countries.

11. **Longest Time Holding Breath Underwater**: Aleix Segura Vendrell of Spain held his breath underwater for 24 minutes and 3 seconds in 2016, showcasing extraordinary human endurance and control.

12. **Most Consecutive Wins in Tennis**: Martina Navratilova holds the record for the most consecutive women's singles matches won, with 74 victories in 1984.

13. **Highest IQ Recorded**: Though IQ tests are controversial and highly debated, Marilyn vos Savant was listed in the Guinness Book of World Records in 1985 for having the highest recorded IQ of 228.

14. **First Person to Climb All 14 Eight-thousanders**: Reinhold Messner was the first person to climb all 14 of the world's peaks over 8,000 meters without the use of supplementary oxygen, completing his last ascent in 1986.

15. **Longest Human Cannonball Flight**: David "The Bullet" Smith Jr. was launched 59.05 meters (193 ft 8.8 in) from a cannon in 2016, setting the record for the longest human cannonball flight.

16. **Most Olympic Gold Medals**: Swimmer Michael Phelps has won the most Olympic gold medals, with a total of 23 golds across four Olympic Games.

17. **Fastest Solar-Powered Vehicle**: The solar-powered car "Sunswift IV" built by students at the University of New South Wales, Australia, set the record for the fastest solar-powered vehicle, reaching a speed of 88.5 km/h (55 mph) in 2011.

18. **Longest Time in Full-Body Ice Contact**: Wim Hof, also known as "The Iceman," holds the record for the longest time in direct, full-body contact with ice, enduring 1 hour, 52 minutes, and 42 seconds.

19. **Deepest Dive Under Ice**: In 2021, Russian diver Konstantin Novikov reached a depth of 102 meters (334 ft 6.96 in) under ice, setting the record for the deepest dive under ice (freshwater).

20. **Longest Continuous Vocal Note**: Richard Fink IV sustained the longest vocal note by a male, holding a note for 2 minutes and 1 second in 2009.

21. **Most Pull-ups in 24 Hours**: John Orth from the United States achieved 7,600 pull-ups in 24 hours in 2016, setting a new world record for endurance and strength.

22. **Fastest 100m in High Heels (Women):** Julia Plecher of Germany ran the 100m in high heels in 14.531 seconds in 2015, combining speed with an unusual challenge.

23. **Most Time Spent in Direct Full-Body Contact with Snow**: In 2013, Jin Songhao of China spent 46 minutes and 7 seconds in direct, full-body contact with snow, setting a chilling record for human endurance.

24. **Fastest Transatlantic Crossing by Rowboat (Team):** In 2011, a team of six rowed across the North Atlantic, from New York to the Isles of Scilly, in 43 days, 21 hours, and 26 minutes, showcasing incredible team endurance and ocean navigation skills.

25. **Longest Spacewalk:** Russian cosmonauts Anatoly Solovyev and Pavel Vinogradov hold the record for the longest spacewalk, lasting 8 hours and 56 minutes during a mission in 1997, demonstrating the extremes of human capability and endurance in space.

These records underscore the remarkable capabilities and resilience of humans, pushing the boundaries of what's physically and mentally possible.

26. **First Successful Ascent of Everest Without Supplemental Oxygen**: In 1978, Reinhold Messner and Peter Habeler made history by climbing Mount Everest without the use of supplemental oxygen, redefining the limits of high-altitude mountaineering.

27. **Deepest Underwater Swim in a Cave**: In 2018, Polish diver Krzysztof Starnawski explored the Hranická Propast, the world's deepest known underwater cave, reaching a depth of 404 meters (1,325 feet).

28. **Fastest Text Message**: In 2005, Sonja Kristiansen of Norway entered the Guinness World Record by typing a 160-character text message in just 37.28 seconds, showcasing the speed of modern communication.

29. **Oldest Person to Climb Everest**: Yuichiro Miura of Japan became the oldest person to summit Mount Everest at the age of 80 in 2013, proving that age is just a number when it comes to pursuing extreme challenges.

30. **Fastest Internet Speed**: In 2020, engineers at University College London achieved a data transmission rate of 178 terabits a second, fast enough to download the entire Netflix library in less than a second.

31. **Longest Basketball Shot**: In 2016, Thunder Law from the Harlem Globetrotters set the record for the longest basketball shot ever made, measuring 34.29 meters (112 feet 6 inches) at the Talking Stick Resort Arena in Phoenix, Arizona.

32. **Most Languages Spoken Fluently**: Ziad Fazah claims to speak 59 different languages fluently, from Arabic to Icelandic to Zulu, showcasing extraordinary linguistic ability.

33. **Longest Time Balancing a Football on the Head**: John Farnworth from the UK set a record for the longest time balancing a football on the head while walking (26.1 km) in 8 hours, 29 minutes, and 46 seconds in 2014.

34. **First Human Genome Sequenced**: In 2003, the Human Genome Project completed the first full sequencing of the human genome, marking a monumental milestone in the fields of genetics and biotechnology.

35. **Longest Human Chain Underwater**: In 2019, 386 divers in Koh Tao, Thailand, formed the longest human chain underwater, highlighting the potential for collective human efforts in raising awareness for ocean conservation.

36. **Fastest Completion of the Seven Summits**: In 2016, Colin O'Brady of the United States completed climbs of the highest peak on each of the seven continents in 132 days, demonstrating remarkable endurance and mountaineering skills.

37. **Longest Plank**: In 2020, George Hood, a former Marine, held a plank position for 8 hours, 15 minutes, and 15 seconds, setting a new world record for core strength and endurance.

38. **Fastest Circumnavigation by Bicycle (Female):** In 2017, British cyclist Jenny Graham circumnavigated the globe by bicycle in 124 days, riding over 18,000 miles and setting a new record for speed and endurance.

39. **Highest Recorded IQ**: William James Sidis (1898–1944) was alleged to have had an IQ between 250 and 300, making him one of the smartest individuals in history, although the exact measure is speculative and not universally recognized due to the lack of standardized testing at the time.

40. **First Person in Space**: Yuri Gagarin, a Soviet cosmonaut, became the first human to travel into space and orbit the Earth on April 12, 1961, marking the beginning of human space exploration.

41. **Fastest Marathon in a Robot Costume**: In 2019, British runner David Smith completed the London Marathon dressed as a robot in 2 hours, 57 minutes, and 43 seconds, blending endurance with creativity.

42. **Longest Duration in Full Body Direct Contact with Ice**: Wim Hof, known as "The Iceman," stayed encased in a block of ice for 1 hour, 52 minutes, and 42 seconds in 2000, demonstrating extraordinary resistance to cold.

43. **Most Pull-Ups in One Minute**: In 2015, Adam Sandel completed 61 pull-ups in one minute, showcasing remarkable strength and stamina.

44. **Fastest to Reach One Million Followers on Instagram**: In 2019, Jennifer Aniston reached one million followers in just 5 hours and 16 minutes after joining the platform, highlighting the power of celebrity influence in the digital age.

45. **First Woman to Win a Nobel Prize**: Marie Curie was the first woman to win a Nobel Prize in 1903 for Physics, and she won another in Chemistry in 1911, making her the first person to win Nobel Prizes in two different scientific fields.

46. **Longest Underwater Walk in One Breath (Female):** In 2016, Marina Kazankova walked 154 meters (505 ft 2.97 in) underwater in a single breath, setting a record for women in freediving endurance and breath-holding.

47. **Most Consecutive Days Running a Marathon Distance:** Between 2015 and 2016, Ricardo Abad from Spain ran a marathon distance (42.195 kilometers / 26.219 miles) for 607 consecutive days, a testament to human physical and mental endurance.

48. **Highest Freefall Parachute Jump:** In 2012, Felix Baumgartner jumped from a helium balloon in the stratosphere at an altitude of 38,969.4 meters (127,852 feet), breaking the sound barrier during his freefall.

49. **First Person to Swim Across the English Channel:** In 1875, Matthew Webb became the first person to swim across the English Channel, covering the distance in 21 hours and 45 minutes, without the use of artificial aids.

50. **Most Goals Scored in a Single Year (Football/Soccer):** In 2012, Lionel Messi set the record for the most goals scored in a calendar year, finding the back of the net 91 times for Barcelona and Argentina.

51. **Deepest Underwater Cycling:** In 2008, Vittorio Innocente set the record for the deepest underwater cycling at 66.5 meters (218 feet), blending the challenges of deep-sea diving with cycling.

52. **Fastest 100m Hurdles Wearing Swim Fins (Female):** In 2008, Veronica Torr of New Zealand set a unique record by completing the 100m hurdles in 22.35 seconds while wearing swim fins, showcasing agility and speed under unconventional conditions.

53. **Longest Time Spent in Direct, Full-body Contact with Snow:** In 2013, Jin Songhao spent 46 minutes and 7 seconds in direct, full-body contact with snow in Yanji, China, demonstrating extreme endurance to cold.

54. **Fastest Completion of All Six World Marathon Majors:** Tim Ferris, an American runner, became the fastest to complete all six World Marathon Majors (Tokyo, Boston, London, Berlin, Chicago, and New York City marathons) in a combined time of just over 10 days in 2019.

55. **Most Weight Lifted by Kettlebell Swings in One Hour:** In 2019, Lorna Biggam from the UK lifted a total of 8,580 kg (18,918 lbs) by kettlebell swings in one hour, setting a record for strength and endurance.

56. **First Double Amputee to Climb Everest**: In 2006, Mark Inglis from New Zealand became the first double amputee to reach the summit of Mount Everest, proving that physical limitations can be overcome with determination and technology.

57. **Longest Continuous Vocal Note (Female):** In 2009, Alpaslan Durmuş from Turkey held a vocal note for 1 minute and 52 seconds, showcasing extraordinary breath control and vocal stamina.

58. **Oldest Person to Complete a Marathon**: In 2011, Fauja Singh from India completed the Toronto Waterfront Marathon at the age of 100, inspiring people worldwide with his fitness and longevity.

59. **Most Consecutive Push-ups Without Breaking Form**: In 1980, Minoru Yoshida of Japan set a record with 10,507 consecutive push-ups, a testament to incredible upper body strength and endurance.

60. **First Solo Flight Around the World Without Refueling**: In 2005, Steve Fossett completed the first solo, nonstop circumnavigation of the Earth in the "Virgin Atlantic GlobalFlyer," covering 36,787.559 kilometers (22,858.729 miles) in 67 hours and 2 minutes.

61. **Deepest Freedive (No Limits):** In 2007, Herbert Nitsch reached a depth of 214 meters (702 feet) in the No Limits freediving category, pushing the limits of human breath-hold diving.

62. **Most Languages Spoken in a Broadcast by a Journalist**: In 2012, Ziad Fazah, fluent in 58 languages, broadcasted live in 41 different languages, showcasing unparalleled linguistic versatility.

63. **Longest Time Living in Isolation**: In 1986, Stefania Follini spent 130 days living alone in an underground cave, with no contact with the outside world, to study human adaptation to isolation.

64. **Longest Time to Maintain a Human Flag**: In 2013, Dominic Lacasse of Canada held a human flag position for 1 minute and 5 seconds, demonstrating exceptional core strength and balance.

65. **Highest Altitude Skydive**: In 2014, Alan Eustace skydived from a helium balloon at an altitude of 41,419 meters (135,890 feet), breaking the sound barrier during his descent.

66. **Fastest Speed on a Skateboard**: In 2016, Kyle Wester reached a speed of 89.41 mph (143.89 km/h) on a skateboard, setting a record for the fastest speed on a skateboard.

67. **Most Math Problems Solved in One Hour**: In 2012, Marc Jornet Sanz solved 3,893 math problems in one hour, demonstrating extraordinary mental calculation ability.

68. **Fastest Time to Climb the Seven Summits Including Both Poles**: In 2011, Parker Liautaud reached the South Pole and the North Pole and summited the highest peaks on all seven continents in 141 days, showcasing remarkable endurance and versatility.

69. **Longest Human Tunnel Travelled Through by a Skateboarding Dog**: In 2015, Otto, a bulldog in Peru, passed through a human tunnel of 30 people on a skateboard, showing not just human but also animal prowess in setting records.

70. **First Person to Walk the Length of the Amazon River**: In 2010, Ed Stafford completed a walk along the Amazon River from its source in Peru to its mouth in Brazil, taking 860 days to cover around 6,992 kilometers (4,345 miles), highlighting human endurance and determination.

71. **Most Times to Summit Everest:** Kami Rita Sherpa of Nepal has summited Mount Everest 24 times as of 2019, the most ascents of the world's highest peak by any individual.

72. **Longest Wingsuit Flight**: In 2016, Jhonathan Florez flew 9.6 kilometers (5.97 miles) in a wingsuit, setting a record for the longest wingsuit flight in terms of distance.

73. **Fastest 100m on a Space Hopper**: In 2013, Ashrita Furman bounced to a new record by completing a 100m dash on a space hopper in 30.2 seconds, adding to his list of multiple unique world records.

74. **First Person to Break the Sound Barrier in Free Fall**: In 2012, Felix Baumgartner jumped from a helium balloon in the stratosphere, reaching a maximum speed of 1,357.64 km/h (843.6 mph), becoming the first person to break the sound barrier outside a vehicle.

75. **Most Grand Slam Tennis Titles Won (Male):** As of 2021, Roger Federer, Rafael Nadal, and Novak Djokovic share the record for the most Grand Slam singles titles won by a male player, each securing 20 titles, showcasing the highest level of achievement in tennis.

.76. **Fastest 100m Hurdles on a Unicycle**: In 2015, Jamey Mossengren from the United States set this unique record, completing the distance in 19.971 seconds and blending the art of unicycling with hurdling.

77. **Longest Time Spent in Direct Contact with Ice (Female):** In 2019, Josefina Monasterio from Venezuela set the female record by remaining encased in ice for 3 hours, and 8 minutes, showcasing incredible mental and physical endurance.

78. **Most People Skiing Down a Slope (Single Day):** In 2015, a record was set in Sochi, Russia, when 1,008 participants skied down a slope simultaneously, celebrating unity and the love for skiing.

79. **Deepest Scuba Dive (Female):** In 2014, Verna van Schaik set the female record for the deepest scuba dive, reaching a depth of 221 meters (725 feet) in Boesmansgat, South Africa, highlighting the extreme capabilities of human endurance and diving technology.

80. **Longest Spaceflight by a Woman**: As of 2020, Christina Koch holds the record for the longest single spaceflight by a woman, spending 328 days aboard the International Space Station, contributing valuable data on the effects of long-duration spaceflight on the human body.

81. **First Woman to Win the Fields Medal**: In 2014, Maryam Mirzakhani from Iran became the first woman to win the Fields Medal, mathematics' highest honor, for her outstanding contributions to the dynamics and geometry of Riemann surfaces and their moduli spaces.

82. **Fastest Speed on a Jet-Powered Bodyboard**: In 2019, Frankie Zapata from France set the record by reaching a speed of 102.8 km/h (63.89 mph) on a jet-powered bodyboard, showcasing innovation in water sports.

83. **Most Consecutive Days Climbing Mt. Everest**: Kami Rita Sherpa of Nepal climbed Everest twice in the 2019 season, bringing his total to 24 ascents, demonstrating unparalleled high-altitude mountaineering skills.

84. **Fastest Solar-Powered Ground Vehicle**: The solar car "Sunswift IV," built by the University of New South Wales in Australia, holds the record for the fastest solar-powered vehicle, reaching a speed of 88.5 km/h (55 mph) in 2011.

85. **Most Goals in a Calendar Year (Football/Soccer):** In 2012, Lionel Messi set the record for most goals in a calendar year, scoring 91 goals for Barcelona and Argentina, showcasing exceptional talent and consistency in football.

86. **Longest Time Spinning a Basketball on a Toothbrush**: In 2019, Sandeep Singh Kaila from Canada set the record by spinning a basketball on a toothbrush held in his mouth for 1 minute and 8.15 seconds, a unique combination of balance and precision.

87. **Oldest Person to Complete an Ironman Triathlon**: Hiromu Inada from Japan became the oldest person to complete an Ironman Triathlon in 2018 at the age of 85 years and 328 days, proving that age is no barrier to extreme endurance sports.

88. **Fastest Mile Run Barefoot on Snow:** In 2020, Jonas Felde Sevaldrud from Norway set the record for the fastest mile run barefoot on snow, clocking in at 5 minutes and 44.72 seconds, highlighting human resilience against cold conditions.

89. **First Person to Complete a Solo Transatlantic Flight**: In 1927, Charles Lindbergh became the first person to fly solo nonstop across the Atlantic Ocean, a monumental achievement in the history of aviation.

90. **Most Times to Summit K2:** As of 2021, Mingma Gyalje Sherpa from Nepal has summited K2, the world's second-highest mountain and one of the most difficult to climb, five times, showcasing extraordinary high-altitude climbing skills.

91. **Longest Apnea with Oxygen (Male):** In 2016, Aleix Segura Vendrell of Spain held his breath underwater for 24 minutes and 3 seconds after inhaling pure oxygen, setting a world record in static apnea.

92. **First Woman in Space**: In 1963, Valentina Tereshkova of the Soviet Union became the first woman to fly in space, orbiting the Earth 48 times and spending almost three days in space, breaking new ground for women in science and exploration.

93. **Longest Time to Balance a Lawnmower on the Chin**: In 2013, Ashrita Furman from the United States balanced a running lawnmower on his chin for 3 minutes and 52 seconds, a record showcasing an unusual combination of balance and courage.

94. **Heaviest Aircraft Pulled by a Man**: In 2009, Kevin Fast from Canada pulled a CC-177 Globemaster III, weighing 188.83 tons (416,299 lbs), a distance of 8.8 meters (28 feet 10.46 inches), demonstrating extraordinary human strength.

95. **Longest Career as a Live Theater Performer:** As of 2021, Philip Astley, who debuted in 1742 and continued performing until he died in 1814, holds the record for the longest career as a live theater performer, spanning over 72 years and influencing the development of modern circus.

96. **Fastest 100m Running on All Fours (Male).** In 2015, Kenichi Ito from Japan set the record for the fastest 100m running on all fours, completing the distance in 15.71 seconds, inspired by the African Patas monkey.

97. **Longest Duration Full Body Contact with Snow (Female):** In 2011, Anna Bågenholm survived after being trapped under ice in freezing water for 80 minutes in Norway, with her body temperature dropping to 13.7°C (56.7°F), the lowest survived body temperature ever recorded.

98. **Deepest Dive in a Submersible**: In 2019, Victor Vescovo descended to a depth of 10,927 meters (35,853 feet) in the Challenger Deep, Mariana Trench, setting a record for the deepest dive in a submersible.

99. **Fastest Rocket-Powered Bicycle:** François Gissy reached a speed of 333 km/h (207 mph) on a rocket-powered bicycle in 2014, blending cycling with rocket science for an unprecedented speed record.

100. **Most Languages Translated for a Book**: The Bible holds the record for being the most translated book, available in parts or whole in over 3,384 languages, demonstrating its universal reach and cultural significance.

Section 2.3: Innovations that Changed the World

Certainly! The impact of inventions on modern society is profound, influencing everything from daily routines to global economies. Here's a detailed look at how certain inventions have shaped the world we live in today:

1. **The Printing Press (1440)**: Invented by Johannes Gutenberg, it revolutionized the way information was disseminated, making books affordable and accessible, which in turn fostered literacy rates and spread knowledge across the globe.

2. **The Steam Engine (1712)**: James Watt's improvements to the steam engine in the late 18th century powered the Industrial Revolution, enabling factories to multiply and cities to grow, fundamentally altering the economic and social fabric of societies.

3. **The Electric Light Bulb (1879):** Thomas Edison's invention illuminated the world, extending work hours beyond daylight and transforming urban landscapes with street lighting, significantly impacting daily life and productivity.

4. **The Telephone (1876)**: Alexander Graham Bell's invention shrank the world, making communication across distances instantaneous and fostering global business and personal connections.

5. **The Automobile (1886):** Karl Benz's motorcar made personal transportation faster and more accessible, leading to the growth of cities, the development of the suburbs, and the shaping of modern landscapes.

6. **The Airplane (1903):** The Wright Brothers' first powered flight turned the world into a global village, making travel and the exchange of goods and ideas faster and more efficient, impacting global cultures and economies.

7. **The Personal Computer (1970s)**: Developed in the 1970s, personal computers democratized access to information, enabling the digital revolution, and transforming how we work, learn, and entertain ourselves.

8. **The Internet (1983):** Originally a project of the U.S. Department of Defense, the Internet has become the backbone of global communication, commerce, and information exchange, reshaping societies and economies.

9. **The World Wide Web (1989):** Tim Berners-Lee's invention provided a user-friendly interface for the Internet, making it accessible to the masses and facilitating the information age.

10. **Mobile Phones (1973):** Martin Cooper's invention, and its evolution into smartphones, have made communication ubiquitous, revolutionizing social interactions, business, and access to infor ma tion.

11. **Vaccination (1796):** Edward Jenner's smallpox vaccine laid the foundation for modern immunology, significantly reducing the impact of infectious diseases on human populations.

12. **Antibiotics (Penicillin, 1928)**: Alexander Fleming's discovery has saved millions of lives by treating bacterial infections, transforming medical practices, and extending life expectancy.

13. **The Refrigerator (1913)**: Domestic refrigerators changed the way we preserve and consume food, impacting health, food distribution, and daily living.

14. **Plastic (1907)**: Leo Baekeland's invention of Bakelite, the first synthetic plastic, paved the way for the vast array of plastic products we rely on today, significantly affecting the environment and manufacturing.

15. **The Assembly Line (1913)**: Pioneered by Henry Ford, it drastically reduced the cost of manufacturing, making goods like automobiles affordable for the masses and transforming industrial production.

16. **Television (1927)**: Philo Farnsworth's invention became a central medium for entertainment and news, shaping public opinion and cultural norms.

17. **GPS Technology (1978)**: Initially developed for military use, GPS has become essential for navigation, and logistics, and has influenced numerous aspects of daily life and commerce.

18. **The ATM (1967)**: The automated teller machine revolutionized banking, making financial transactions instantaneous and convenient, altering consumer behavior and banking operations.

19. **The Digital Camera (1975)**: Invented by Steve Sasson, digital photography has transformed how we capture, share, and store memories, impacting media, entertainment, and personal communication.

20. **Social Media Platforms (Early 2000s)**: Sites like Facebook and Twitter have reshaped social interactions, marketing, and the dissemination of information, influencing politics, culture, and individual relationships.

21. **The Microwave Oven (1946)**: Percy Spencer's invention changed cooking methods, making food preparation quicker and more convenient, and influencing culinary habits and lifestyles.

22. **The Transistor (1947)**: This invention revolutionized electronics, making it possible to develop smaller, more efficient devices like computers, radios, and televisions, impacting technology and society.

23. **E-commerce (1990s):** The rise of online shopping platforms like Amazon has transformed retail, affecting global commerce, consumer habits, and the economy.

24. **Renewable Energy Technologies (20th Century):** Innovations in solar and wind energy are pivotal in addressing climate change, influencing global energy policies, and promoting sustainable development.

25. **Blockchain Technology and Cryptocurrency (2008):** Introduced with Bitcoin, blockchain technology has the potential to revolutionize financial transactions, ensuring security and transparency, impacting banking, law, and beyond.

These inventions illustrate the profound impact of human ingenuity on shaping modern society, affecting how we live, work, and interact with our world and each other.

26. **The Internet of Things (IoT) (1999):** The concept of connecting everyday objects to the internet, allowing them to send and receive data, is revolutionizing industries, smart homes, and healthcare, making environments more responsive and efficient.

27. **3D Printing (1980s):** This technology allows for the layer-by-layer creation of objects, revolutionizing manufacturing, prototyping, and even medicine, by enabling custom solutions and on-demand production.

28. **Artificial Intelligence (AI) and Machine Learning (1950s-1980s):** These technologies are at the forefront of the fourth industrial revolution, transforming business processes, enhancing decision-making, and personalizing user experiences across sectors.

29. **High-speed Rail (1964):** First introduced in Japan as the Shinkansen, or "bullet train," high-speed rail networks have significantly reduced travel times between cities, promoting economic growth and environmental sustainability.

30. **The Lithium-Ion Battery (1991):** This rechargeable battery technology powers a vast array of portable electronics, and electric vehicles, and is critical to the storage of renewable energy, facilitating the transition to cleaner power sources.

31. **Wireless Communication (Late 19th Century):** The development of radio, and later technologies like Wi-Fi and Bluetooth, has made remote communication and data transfer commonplace, supporting the proliferation of mobile devices and the internet.

32. **The Contraceptive Pill (1960)**: This invention provided unprecedented control over reproductive health, contributing significantly to gender equality, personal freedom, and societal changes.

33. **Genetic Engineering (1973)**: Techniques for manipulating the DNA of organisms have led to advances in agriculture, medicine, and biotechnology, offering solutions to food security, genetic diseases, and environmental challenges.

34. **CRISPR Gene Editing (2012)**: This precise method for editing DNA is a groundbreaking tool in medical research, with potential applications in treating genetic disorders, eradicating diseases, and improving food crops.

35. **Satellite Technology (1957)**: Since the launch of Sputnik, satellites have become indispensable for communication, navigation, weather forecasting, and earth observation, influencing global connectivity and our understanding of the planet.

36. **The Global Positioning System (GPS) (1978)**: Initially developed for military navigation, GPS has become essential for civilian applications, transforming navigation, and logistics, and even enabling new technologies like autonomous vehicles.

37. **Digital Music (1980s)**: The shift from physical to digital formats has transformed how we consume music, giving rise to streaming services and changing the landscape of the music industry.

38. **Quantum Computing (Ongoing)**: Though still in its infancy, quantum computing promises to revolutionize fields by performing complex calculations at unprecedented speeds, potentially transforming cryptography, drug discovery, and more.

39. **The Silicon Chip (1958)**: The invention of the integrated circuit, or silicon chip, by Jack Kilby and Robert Noyce, miniaturized electronics and is foundational to all modern electronic devices.

40. **The Human Genome Project (Completed 2003)**: Mapping the entire human genome has advanced our understanding of genetics, disease, and evolution, paving the way for personalized medicine and biotechnological breakthroughs.

41. **LED Lighting (1962)**: Light-emitting diodes (LEDs) have transformed lighting by being more energy-efficient and longer-lasting than traditional bulbs, significantly reducing energy consumption worldwide.

42. **E-mail (1971)**: The development of electronic mail revolutionized communication, making it instantaneous and accessible, changing the landscape of personal and professional interactions.

43. **Smartphones (2007)**: The introduction of the smartphone has combined numerous technologies into one device, revolutionizing communication, entertainment, and internet access, and becoming an indispensable part of daily life.

44. **Cloud Computing (2006)**: This technology has democratized access to computing resources and data storage, enabling scalable services, fostering innovation, and supporting the exponential growth of the Internet economy.

45. **Social Networking Sites (2004)**: Platforms like Facebook have transformed social interactions, marketing, and the dissemination of information, influencing politics, culture, and individual rela tionships.

46. **Virtual Reality (VR) and Augmented Reality (AR) (2010s)**: These technologies are creating immersive experiences in gaming, education, and training, offering new ways to interact with digital environments.

47. **Blockchain Technology (2008)**: Beyond cryptocurrencies, blockchain offers a secure and transparent way to conduct transactions and share information, with potential impacts on various sectors including finance, healthcare, and governance.

48. **Online Learning Platforms (Late 1990s)**: The rise of e-learning has transformed education, making knowledge more accessible and supporting lifelong learning and flexible educational oppor tunities.

49. **Digital Currency and Cryptocurrency (2009)**: Bitcoin and subsequent cryptocurrencies have challenged traditional financial systems, offering a decentralized approach to banking and transactions.

50. **Renewable Energy Technologies (Late 20th Century)**: Advances in solar, wind, and hydroelectric technologies are pivotal in combating climate change, reducing reliance on fossil fuels, and promoting sustainable development.

These innovations underscore the dynamic nature of technological progress and its wide-ranging impact on society, economy, and daily life, continually reshaping our world in unforeseen ways.

Certainly! Continuing with the exploration of inventions and technologies that have significantly impacted modern society, here are more innovations:

51. **Self-driving Cars (21st Century)**: Autonomous vehicle technology, combining AI, sensors, and software, promises to revolutionize transportation, reduce accidents, and transform urban planning.

52. **Solar Panels (1954)**: The development of photovoltaic cells for converting sunlight into electricity has been crucial for the adoption of renewable energy, reducing carbon emissions and dependence on fossil fuels.

53. **The Barcode (1952)**: This system of representing data in a visual, machine-readable form revolutionized inventory management, speeding up checkout processes and transforming retail and lo gistics.

54. **Fiber Optic Communications (1970s)**: This technology, transmitting information as light pulses along glass or plastic fibers, has greatly increased the speed and capacity of telecommunications, enabling high-speed internet and global connectivity.

55. **Drones (21st Century)**: Initially developed for military use, drones have found applications in civilian life, including aerial photography, agriculture, delivery services, and environmental monitoring.

56. **Wind Turbines (1887)**: Modern wind turbines harness wind energy to generate electricity, contributing significantly to renewable energy sources and helping to reduce greenhouse gas emissions.

57. **The Electric Guitar (1931)**: This instrument revolutionized music, giving rise to new genres like rock and roll and reshaping cultural landscapes.

58. **Contact Lenses (1887)**: These small lenses worn directly on the eyes have provided an alternative to eyeglasses, improving vision and lifestyle for millions.

59. **The Space Telescope (Hubble, 1990)**: Placing telescopes in space, free from atmospheric distortion, has vastly expanded our understanding of the universe, enabling the observation of distant galaxies, black holes, and other cosmic phenomena.

60. **Digital Video Recorders (DVR) (1999)**: DVR technology has changed the way people watch television, allowing users to record, pause, and rewind live TV, influencing viewing habits and the television industry.

61. **In Vitro Fertilization (IVF) (1978)**: This medical technique has provided couples with fertility issues the chance to have children, significantly impacting reproductive medicine and ethical discussions.

62. **Nanotechnology (1980s)**: The manipulation of matter on an atomic or molecular scale has potential applications in medicine, electronics, and materials science, promising to bring about significant technological advancements.

63. **3D Printing in Medicine (21st Century)**: The use of 3D printing to produce medical devices, prosthetics, and even organ tissues is revolutionizing healthcare, offering personalized medical solutions, and advancing surgical practices.

64. **Wearable Technology (2010s)**: Devices like smartwatches and fitness trackers have integrated technology into daily life, monitoring health, facilitating communication, and enhancing convenience.

65. **Smart Home Devices (21st Century)**: Technology that automates home systems—ranging from lighting to security—has improved energy efficiency, security, and convenience, contributing to the concept of the "Internet of Things."

66. **Augmented Reality (AR) in Retail (2010s)**: AR technology enhances the shopping experience by allowing customers to visualize products in real time, improving engagement and personalizing the retail experience.

67. **Electric Aircraft (21st Century)**: While still in early development, electric propulsion for aircraft promises to reduce greenhouse gas emissions and noise, potentially transforming air travel into a more sustainable mode of transportation.

68. **Biodegradable Plastics (Late 20th Century)**: Developed to reduce pollution and reliance on fossil fuels, biodegradable plastics decompose naturally, offering an environmentally friendly alternative to traditional plastics.

69. **Hydraulic Fracturing (1947)**: This technique for extracting oil and gas from shale rock has significantly increased energy production but also sparked environmental and health concerns, influencing the global energy market and policies.

70. **The Synthetic Genome (2010)**: Scientists created the first synthetic bacterial genome, paving the way for advances in synthetic biology, with potential applications in medicine, biofuel production, and environmental remediation.

71. **Voice Assistants (2010s)**: AI-powered voice recognition technology has given rise to virtual assistants, making technology more accessible and integrating seamlessly into daily tasks and routines.

72. **Smart Cities (21st Century)**: The integration of information and communication technologies into urban infrastructure aims to improve the efficiency of services, reduce waste and costs, and enhance citizens' quality of life.

73. **Graphene (2004)**: Since its isolation, this form of carbon, known for its extraordinary strength, conductivity, and flexibility, has potential applications in electronics, materials science, and energy storage.

74. **The Electric Vehicle (EV) Revolution (2000s)**: The rise of EVs, led by companies like Tesla, is driving a shift towards sustainable transportation, reducing reliance on fossil fuels and emissions of greenhouse gases.

75. **Robotic Surgery (2000s)**: Robotic systems have enhanced the precision and capabilities of surgeons, reducing recovery times and improving outcomes in various types of surgery.

76. **Precision Agriculture (Early 21st Century)**: Leveraging GPS, IoT devices, and AI, precision agriculture allows farmers to increase efficiency and crop yields while minimizing waste and environmental impact, revolutionizing food production.

77. **Quantum Encryption (21st Century)**: This emerging technology promises unbreakable encryption for secure communication, leveraging the principles of quantum mechanics, and has the potential to redefine cybersecurity.

78. **Artificial Organs (21st Century)**: Advances in bioengineering and 3D printing have led to the development of artificial organs, offering new hope for patients awaiting transplants and pushing the boundaries of medical science.

79. **The Smart Grid (21st Century)**: An electricity supply network that uses digital communications technology to detect and react to local changes in usage, improving the efficiency and reliability of electricity distribution.

80. **High-Efficiency Photovoltaic Cells (21st Century)**: Continued advancements in solar cell technology have significantly improved the efficiency and affordability of solar power, accelerating the transition to renewable energy.

81. **Blockchain in Supply Chain Management (2010s)**: By providing a transparent and secure method to track the production, shipment, and receipt of products, blockchain technology has the potential to revolutionize supply chain management.

82. **Gesture Recognition Technology (2010s)**: This technology allows users to interact with devices through gestures by using sensors and advanced algorithms, enhancing user interfaces in gaming, automotive, and smart home devices.

83. **Biometric Verification (Late 20th Century)**: The use of unique physiological characteristics, such as fingerprints or facial features, for identification, has enhanced security in digital and physical spaces, impacting law enforcement, border control, and personal device access.

84. **Digital Assistive Technologies (21st Century)**: Innovations such as screen readers, speech-to-text, and specialized input devices have made technology more accessible, empowering individuals with disabilities to participate more fully in society.

85. **Neural Networks and Deep Learning (2010s)**: These AI methodologies mimic the workings of the human brain to interpret complex data patterns, revolutionizing fields from computer vision to natural language processing.

86. **The Large Hadron Collider (2008)**: The world's largest and most powerful particle accelerator has pushed the boundaries of particle physics, unlocking secrets of the universe and contributing to our understanding of the fundamental structure of matter.

87. **Wireless Charging (21st Century)**: This technology allows electronic devices to be charged without cables, enhancing convenience and leading to the development of more integrated and waterproof devices.

88. **Lab-grown Meat (21st Century)**: Cultivating meat from animal cells without raising and slaughtering animals could significantly reduce the environmental impact of meat production and address ethical concerns about animal welfare.

89. **Smart Glasses and Augmented Reality Headsets (2010s)**: Devices that overlay digital information onto the physical world have applications in education, manufacturing, and entertainment, potentially revolutionizing how we interact with information and our environment.

90. **Waste-to-Energy Technologies (21st Century):** Converting municipal and industrial waste into electricity and heat offers a sustainable waste management solution while contributing to energy production, reducing landfill use, and cutting greenhouse gas emissions.

91. **Digital Twin Technology (2010s)**: Creating virtual replicas of physical systems to simulate, predict, and control their behavior in real time can enhance efficiency in manufacturing, urban planning, and healthcare.

92. **Wearable Medical Devices (21st Century):** From fitness trackers to continuous glucose monitors, wearable devices have transformed healthcare by enabling real-time, personalized monitoring and data collection.

93. **Adaptive Learning Technology (21st Century)**: AI-driven educational platforms that adjust to individual learning styles and paces, improving educational outcomes and personalizing learning experiences.

94. **Space Tourism (21st Century)**: Pioneered by companies like SpaceX and Virgin Galactic, space tourism aims to make space travel accessible to non-astronauts, marking the beginning of a new era in space exploration.

95. **Ocean Thermal Energy Conversion (OTEC) (21st Century***: This technology exploits temperature differences between ocean surface water and deeper layers to generate renewable energy, offering a potential source of clean power for coastal regions.

96. **Nano-medicine (21st Century)**: The application of nanotechnology in medicine offers potential breakthroughs in diagnosing, treating, and preventing diseases by operating at the molecular level.

97. **5G Technology (2019)**: The fifth generation of cellular network technology provides faster speeds, lower latency, and the capacity to connect more devices simultaneously, enabling advancements in smart cities, autonomous vehicles, and augmented reality.

98. **Biodegradable Electronics (21st Century):** Developing electronic components that can safely decompose in the environment addresses the growing problem of electronic waste, promoting sustainability.

99. **Brain-Computer Interfaces (BCIs) (21st Century):** BCIs connect the human brain to external devices, allowing for direct communication between the brain and computers, with potential applications in medicine, communication, and control of machines.

100. **Synthetic Biology (21st Century):** The redesign of biological systems for new purposes, such as biofuel production, pollution control, and the creation of new biological parts, devices, and systems, stands to reshape industries and environmental management.

These facts further illustrate the incredible pace of innovation and its profound impact on nearly every aspect of modern life, from healthcare and energy to communication and entertainment, highlighting the endless possibilities that technology holds for the future.

Chapter 3: Mind-Boggling Science and Technology

Section 3.1: Quantum Quirks

Quantum mechanics, a fundamental theory in physics that provides a description of the physical properties of nature at the scale of atoms and subatomic particles, is notoriously complex. Here are 25 facts aimed at simplifying its complexities:

1. **Quantum mechanics explores the behavior of particles at the smallest scales**. It describes how things work differently at the atomic and subatomic levels compared to what we observe in our everyday lives.

2. **Particles can exist in multiple states simultaneously**. This is known as superposition. For example, an electron can be in multiple places at once until it is observed.

3. **Observation affects quantum systems.** The act of measuring a quantum state can change it, a phenomenon famously illustrated by Schrödinger's cat thought experiment.

4. **Quantum entanglement is a strong correlation between particles.** Once particles are entangled, the state of one (no matter the distance from the other) can instantly affect the state of the other.

5. **Energy is quantized**. This means that energy exists in discrete "packets" rather than being continuous, leading to the idea that light can act as both a wave and a particle (photon).

6. **The Heisenberg Uncertainty Principle states that you cannot simultaneously know the exact position and momentum of a particle.** The more accurately you know one, the less accurately you can know the other.

7. **Quantum tunneling allows particles to pass through barriers.** This occurs even if the particles do not have enough energy to do so under classical physics, a principle used in technologies like tunneling microscopes and semiconductors.

8. **Wave-particle duality is a core concept of quantum mechanics.** Particles like electrons and photons exhibit properties of both particles and waves.

9. **Quantum mechanics is probabilistic**. It deals with probabilities rather than certainties, predicting the likelihood of finding a particle in a particular state.

10. **The Pauli Exclusion Principle states that no two fermions (like electrons) can occupy the same quantum state simultaneously.** This principle explains a wide range of physical phenomena, including the structure of the periodic table and the stability of matter.

11. **Quantum superconductivity occurs when materials conduct electricity with zero resistance at very low temperatures.** This phenomenon has potential applications in magnetic levitation and lossless electrical transmission.

12. **Quantum computing uses the principles of quantum mechanics to process information in ways that classical computers cannot**. This includes solving certain types of problems much more efficiently.

13. **The double-slit experiment demonstrates that light and matter can display characteristics of both classically defined waves and particles**. The outcome of the experiment changes dramatically when observed, illustrating the fundamental principles of quantum mechanics.

14. **Quantum cryptography uses quantum mechanical properties to secure data transmission.** It promises theoretically unbreakable encryption methods.

15. **The Copenhagen interpretation is one of the oldest and most widely accepted interpretations of quantum mechanics.** It suggests that quantum particles don't have definite states unless they're being observed.

16. **Quantum field theory combines quantum mechanics with special relativity.** It provides the framework for understanding particle physics and the forces of nature.

17. **The Many-Worlds Interpretation suggests that all possible outcomes of quantum measurements are physically realized in some "world" or universe.**

18. **Quantum mechanics has led to the invention of technologies such as lasers, transistors, and MRI machines.**

19. **The concept of spin in quantum mechanics refers to the intrinsic angular momentum of particles.** Spin is a quantum property without a classical analog.

20. **Quantum decoherence is a process by which quantum systems lose their quantum properties as they interact with their environment.** It is a key factor in why we don't observe quantum behavior in everyday objects.

21. **The Schrödinger equation is the fundamental equation of quantum mechanics.** It describes how the quantum state of a physical system changes over time.

22. **Quantum mechanics challenges the concept of determinism.** Because of its probabilistic nature, it implies that events at a quantum level can't be predicted with absolute cer tainty.

23. **Virtual particles are particles that exist in a quantum field for a short time and interval**. They are a consequence of the uncertainty principle and have real effects, such as the Casimir effect.

24. **The pilot-wave theory, or Bohmian mechanics, offers an alternative to the standard interpretation of quantum mechanics.** It suggests that particles have defined paths determined by a guiding wave.

25. **Quantum entanglement challenges the notion of locality**. It suggests that particles can be connected in such a way that the state of one (regardless of distance) can instantaneously affect the state of another.

26. **Quantum Fluctuations:** In the vacuum of space, particles, and antiparticles spontaneously appear and then annihilate each other, a process driven by the uncertainty principle.

27. **Planck's Constant (h):** A fundamental quantity in quantum mechanics that sets the scale for action in the quantum realm, highlighting the discrete nature of energy exchange.

28. **Quantum Zeno Effect:** The phenomenon where a quantum system can be prevented from evolving by measuring it frequently, essentially "freezing" its state.

29. **Quantum Eraser Experiment:** This experiment demonstrates that when information about a particle's path is erased, the quantum behavior of the system can be restored, challenging classical notions of information and causality.

30. **Bell's Theorem**: It provides a test for quantum entanglement and shows that no local theory of classical physics can reproduce all the predictions of quantum mechanics.

31. **No-Cloning Theorem**: In quantum mechanics, it is impossible to create an exact copy of an arbitrary unknown quantum state, a principle that underpins quantum cryptography.

32. **Quantum Teleportation:** The process by which the state of a quantum system can be transmitted from one location to another, with the help of classical communication and a previously shared quantum entanglement.

33. **Aharonov-Bohm Effect**: Demonstrates that electric and magnetic fields can influence the phase of a particle's wave function, even in regions where the field strength is zero, underscoring the fundamental role of potentials in quantum mechanics.

34. **Quantum Chromodynamics (QCD):** The theory that describes the strong force (one of the four fundamental forces), governing the interactions between quarks and gluons, particles that make up protons and neutrons.

35. **Superposition Principle:** The principle that any quantum system can exist in multiple states simultaneously until it is observed, at which point it 'collapses' into one of its possible sta tes.

36. **Wave Function Collapse**: The process by which a quantum system's wave function, representing a superposition of states, becomes a single definite state upon measurement.

37. **De Broglie Wavelength**: The idea that every moving particle or object has an associated wave, blending classical and quantum concepts by suggesting wave-particle duality applies not just to photons, but to all matter.

38. **Quantum Hall Effect**: A quantum mechanical phenomenon in which the conductivity of electrons forms quantized plateaus at low temperatures and strong magnetic fields, providing a precise standard for electrical resistance.

39. **Feynman Path Integral:** A formulation of quantum mechanics that sums over all possible paths a particle can take, offering a unique perspective on quantum phenomena.

40. **Quantum Computing Qubits**: Unlike classical bits, which can be 0 or 1, qubits can be in a state of 0, 1, or a superposition of both, enabling quantum computers to solve certain problems much more efficiently than classical computers.

41. **Quantum Annealing**: A quantum algorithm for solving optimization problems by exploiting quantum superposition and tunneling to find the minimum of a function.

42. **Topological Quantum Computing**: A theoretical quantum computing model that uses quasiparticles called anyons, whose paths around each other can encode quantum information in a way that is resistant to errors.

43. **Quantum Supremacy**: The point at which a quantum computer can perform a calculation that is impractical for classical computers, demonstrating the superior potential of quantum computa tion.

44. **Quantum Entropy**: A measure of the uncertainty or disorder within a quantum system, playing a crucial role in quantum information theory and thermodynamics.

45. **Quantum Coherence**: The property of a quantum system that allows for the interference of probabilities associated with its state, fundamental for quantum computing and quantum cryptography.

46. **Quantum Discord:** A measure of the non-classical correlations between parts of a quantum system, going beyond entanglement to capture a broader range of quantum phenomena.

47. **Quantum Optics:** The study of how quantum mechanics affects the behavior of light and its interaction with matter, leading to applications such as lasers and quantum cryptography.

48. **Weak Measurement**: A type of quantum measurement that slightly disturbs the system, allowing for certain properties to be measured without causing a significant collapse of the wave function.

49. **Quantum Simulation:** Using a quantum system to model another quantum system that is difficult to study directly, potentially unlocking new materials, drugs, and understanding of fundamental processes.

50. **Bose-Einstein Condensate (BEC):** A state of matter formed at near absolute zero temperatures where a group of atoms is cooled to near absolute zero, causing them to occupy the same space and quantum state, effectively behaving as a single quantum entity.

These additional facts offer a glimpse into the depth and breadth of quantum mechanics, highlighting its principles, paradoxes, and the revolutionary technologies it has inspired, each contributing to our ever-evolving understanding of the universe at its most fundamental level.

Section 3.3: **The AI Revolution**

Artificial intelligence (AI) is increasingly becoming a fundamental part of everyday life, transforming industries, enhancing services, and shaping how we interact with the world. Here are 25 insightful facts on how AI is making an impact:

1. **Personalized Recommendations**: AI algorithms analyze your browsing and purchasing history to recommend products, services, and content tailored to your preferences, seen in platforms like Amazon and Netflix.

2. **Smart Home Devices**: Devices like thermostats, lights, and security cameras use AI to learn from your habits and preferences, automating tasks to enhance convenience and efficiency.

3. **Virtual Assistants**: Siri, Alexa, and Google Assistant use AI to understand natural language, making it possible to control devices, set reminders, and obtain information through voice commands.

4. **Autonomous Vehicles**: AI is at the core of self-driving car technology, enabling vehicles to interpret sensor data to identify objects, make decisions, and navigate roads with minimal human intervention.

5. **Healthcare Diagnostics**: AI algorithms help doctors diagnose diseases more accurately and quickly by analyzing medical images, such as X-rays and MRIs, for signs of diseases like cancer.

6. **Predictive Text and Autocorrect**: AI powers the predictive text and autocorrect features on smartphones, learning from your typing habits to improve accuracy and speed in communica tion.

7. **Fraud Detection:** Financial institutions use AI to analyze transaction patterns and flag potentially fraudulent activities, significantly reducing the risk of financial fraud.

8. **Robotic Process Automation (RPA):** AI is used in automating repetitive tasks in various industries, from data entry and analysis to customer service, improving efficiency and accuracy.

9. **Language Translation**: Tools like Google Translate use AI to provide real-time, accurate translation between languages, breaking down language barriers in communication.

10. **E-commerce Search Engines:** AI enhances the search functionality on e-commerce platforms, understanding user queries to deliver relevant search results and product suggestions.

11. **Educational Tool**: AI-powered platforms provide personalized learning experiences, adapting to each student's learning pace and style, improving engagement and outcomes.

12. **Agriculture**: AI technologies help in monitoring crop health, predicting weather patterns, and automating tasks like watering and harvesting, leading to increased efficiency and yield.

13. **Smart Cities.** AI is used to manage traffic flow, optimize public transportation, and improve energy efficiency in cities, enhancing urban living.

14. **Environmental Monitoring:** AI assists in tracking and predicting environmental changes, such as air quality and deforestation, contributing to conservation efforts.

15. **Sports Analytics**: Coaches and athletes use AI for performance analysis, injury prediction, and game strategy development, enhancing training and competition strategies.

16. **Customer Service Chatbots:** AI-driven chatbots provide instant customer service across many websites, handling inquiries and solving problems around the clock.

17. **Facial Recognition**: Used in security and surveillance, AI-powered facial recognition technology can identify individuals in crowds or unlock personal devices.

18. **Content Creation**: AI tools assist in generating articles, reports, and marketing copy, streamlining content creation processes.

19. **Social Media Monitoring**: AI algorithms analyze social media content to identify trends, monitor brand mentions, and understand consumer sentiment.

20. **Fitness and Health Tracking**: Wearables use AI to analyze physical activity, monitor health metrics, and provide personalized fitness coaching.

21. **Supply Chain Optimization**: AI optimizes logistics, forecasting demand, and managing inventory in real-time, reducing costs and improving efficiency.

22. **Music and Media Composition**: AI algorithms generate music, video game content, and even art, pushing the boundaries of creativity and entertainment.

23. **Disaster Prediction and Response**: AI helps predict natural disasters, such as hurricanes and earthquakes, improving preparedness and response efforts.

24. **Legal Document Analysis**: AI tools assist lawyers by quickly analyzing legal documents for pertinent information, saving time and improving accuracy in legal reviews.

25. **Energy Management**: AI optimizes energy consumption in homes and businesses, contributing to sustainability by reducing energy waste and managing renewable energy sources.

These insights demonstrate AI's pervasive influence across various aspects of daily life, significantly enhancing efficiency, convenience, and decision-making processes.

The integration of artificial intelligence (AI) continues to revolutionize daily life, industry operations, and societal functions in profound ways. Here are more insightful facts about how AI is further transforming the world:

26. **Real-time Language Interpretation**: AI powers devices and applications that offer real-time spoken language interpretation, facilitating cross-lingual conversations and making global business and travel more accessible.

27. **Smart Retail:** From personalized shopping experiences to inventory management, AI is reshaping retail, enabling stores to predict trends, optimize staffing, and enhance customer sa tisfaction.

28. **Autonomous Drones:** AI enables drones to navigate autonomously, and perform tasks like delivery, agricultural monitoring, and search and rescue operations more efficiently.

29. **Augmented Reality (AR) Experiences**: AI algorithms process real-world data to enhance AR applications, creating immersive experiences in gaming, education, and retail.

30. **Predictive Maintenance:** In manufacturing and transportation, AI predicts when machines are likely to fail or need maintenance, significantly reducing downtime and operational costs.

31. **AI in Filmmaking**: From script analysis to post-production, AI tools are being used to streamline filmmaking processes, enhance visual effects, and even predict box office success.

32. **Mental Health Support**: AI-powered applications provide mental health support, offering therapy chatbots and mood tracking to help manage conditions like anxiety and depression.

33. **Customized News Feeds:** AI curates personalized news experiences, analyzing reading habits to deliver content aligned with individual interests and preferences.

34. **AI in Gaming**: Beyond enhancing graphics and gameplay, AI is used to create dynamic, responsive environments and non-player characters that adapt to player actions.

35. **Public Safety and Security**: AI enhances public safety through advanced surveillance systems, anomaly detection, and automated emergency response coordination.

36. **Weather Forecasting:** AI improves the accuracy of weather predictions by analyzing vast datasets more efficiently than traditional methods, aiding disaster preparedness and agricultural planning.

37. **Intelligent Transportation Systems**: AI optimizes traffic management and public transport scheduling, reducing congestion and enhancing commuter experiences.

38. **Personal Finance Management**: AI-powered tools assist individuals in managing their finances, from budgeting to investments, providing personalized advice and predictions.

39. **Remote Monitoring and Healthcare:** AI enables remote patient monitoring, analyzing data from wearable devices to offer real-time insights into patient health and predict potential issues.

40. **Digital Art and Design**: AI tools are transforming the creative industries, enabling artists and designers to experiment with generative art, automate tedious processes, and explore new forms of creativity.

41. **Ethical AI and Governance:** As AI becomes more embedded in daily life, efforts are increasing to ensure AI systems are developed and deployed ethically, with a focus on fairness, transparency, and accountability.

42. **Voice-to-Text Evolution:** AI has significantly improved voice-to-text technologies, enhancing accuracy and understanding across different languages and accents, and making digital communication more accessible.

43. **AI in Archaeology:** AI tools analyze satellite images and historical data to predict archaeological site locations, revolutionizing the way historical research and excavations are conducted.

44. **Enhanced Network Security**: AI algorithms identify and respond to cyber threats in real time, improving the security of digital infrastructure and sensitive data.

45. **AI for Environmental Conservation**: AI aids in tracking wildlife, analyzing ecosystem changes, and modeling climate change impacts, contributing to conservation efforts and sustainable development.

46. **Precision Agriculture**: AI optimizes farming practices, analyzing data on soil conditions, crop health, and weather to maximize yield and reduce resource use.

47. **Customized Learning Platforms**: AI-driven educational platforms adapt to individual learning styles, pacing, and needs, offering customized curricula and improving educational outcomes.

48. **Automated Video Editing**: AI simplifies video production, automating editing processes, enhancing video quality, and generating content based on user preferences.

49. **AI in Space Exploration**: From analyzing astronomical data to autonomously navigating rovers on Mars, AI plays a crucial role in advancing space exploration and study.

50. **Quantum Computing and AI:** The integration of AI with emerging quantum computing technologies promises to unlock new potentials in processing speed and problem-solving capabilities, potentially revolutionizing fields such as cryptography, materials science, and complex system simulation.

These additional insights underscore the expansive and accelerating influence of AI across various facets of life and work, heralding a future where AI's integration is seamless and universally beneficial.

Chapter 4: Secrets of the Past

Section 4.1: Ancient Civilizations

Unraveling the mysteries of ancient societies and their innovations offers a fascinating glimpse into the genius of early civilizations. These societies laid the groundwork for many modern technologies and concepts, demonstrating incredible ingenuity without access to the tools and information we have today. Here are facts highlighting their remarkable contributions:

1. **The Pyramids of Egypt**: The construction of the Pyramids, especially the Great Pyramid of Giza around 2580–2560 BC, remains one of the greatest architectural achievements, using advanced mathematics and astronomy.

2. **Sumerian Cuneiform Writing**: Developed around 3400 BC in Mesopotamia, cuneiform writing is one of the earliest known systems of writing, evidencing the complexity of communication in ancient societies.

3. **The Antikythera Mechanism**: This ancient Greek device, dated to about 100 BC, is the world's oldest known analog computer, used to predict astronomical positions and eclipses for calendrical and astrological purposes.

4. **Roman Concrete:** Ancient Romans created a durable concrete that has withstood the test of time, outlasting modern concrete in many cases. Structures like the Pantheon's dome are still standing after nearly 2000 years.

5. **The Aqueducts of Rome**: Romans engineered extensive aqueduct systems in the 1st century BC, delivering fresh water to urban centers from distant sources, a critical innovation in urban infrastructure.

6. **The Terracotta Army:** Dating back to 210–209 BC, this collection of terracotta sculptures depicting the armies of Qin Shi Huang, the first Emperor of China, showcases advanced craftsmanship and mass production methods.

7. **Mayan Astronomy**: The Mayan civilization, notable from 2000 BC to AD 1500, had an advanced understanding of astronomy, developing a complex calendar system that accurately tracked celestial movements.

8. **Ancient Indian Metallurgy**: The Delhi iron pillar, dating back to 400 AD, demonstrates advanced ancient Indian knowledge of metallurgy, showing little to no signs of corrosion after more than 1600 years.

9. **The Library of Alexandria**: Founded in the 3rd century BC in Egypt, it was one of the largest and most significant libraries of the ancient world, symbolizing the thirst for knowledge and scholarly pursuits.

10. **The Incan Road System:** Spanning over 40,000 kilometers, the Incan road system facilitated communication, trade, and military movement across the Incan Empire, showcasing sophisticated engineering skills.

11. **Chinese Paper Making**: Invented in the 2nd century BC by Cai Lun, paper making marked a revolution in recording information, replacing cumbersome materials like silk and bamboo.

12. **The Phoenician Alphabet:** Developed around 1050 BC, the Phoenician alphabet is considered the ancestor of most modern alphabets, greatly simplifying the process of writing and reading.

13. **Ancient Greek Fire:** A weapon used by the Byzantine Empire, Greek fire was a closely guarded state secret that could continue burning even on water, demonstrating advanced chemical knowledge.

14. **Baghdad Battery**: Dating back to the Parthian or Sassanid periods, these clay jars contained iron and copper and are believed by some to have been used as a galvanic cell for electroplating, though this is debated.

15. **Ancient Surgery:** The Sushruta Samhita, written in India during the 6th century BC, describes surgical techniques and instruments, showcasing early advances in medical knowledge.

16. **Mesoamerican Rubber:** The Olmecs, living in present-day Mexico from about 1600–350 BC, were the first to make rubber from latex, using it for balls, bands, and figurines.

17. **The South Pointing Chariot**: This ancient Chinese invention used differential gearing to keep a figure pointing south, regardless of the chariot's direction, an early use of gears for navigation.

18. **Ancient Egyptian Medicine**: The Ebers Papyrus, dating back to 1550 BC, contains over 700 remedies and treatments, illustrating sophisticated medical practices.

19. **The Astrolabe**: Used by ancient astronomers and navigators, the astrolabe, developed in the Hellenistic world in about 150 BC, could measure the altitude of stars and planets to determine local latitude and time.

20. **Norse Longships**: These advanced sailing vessels, developed by the Vikings during the 9th century, enabled them to navigate across the open sea, reaching as far as North America.

21. **Hydraulic Engineering of Angkor Wat**: The Khmer Empire, between the 9th and 15th centuries, constructed an elaborate system of water management that supported large-scale agriculture and the population.

22. **The Windmill**: First recorded in Persia in AD 500–900, windmills were used for grinding grain and pumping water, an early adaptation of wind energy.

23. **Zero in Mathematics**: The concept of zero as a number was developed by ancient Indian mathematicians around the 5th century AD, a fundamental breakthrough in mathematics.

24. **Ancient Cartography:** The Babylonian Map of the World, dating back to the 5th century BC, represents one of the earliest known maps, showing how ancient civilizations perceived their world.

25. **Roman Roads:** The Roman Empire built an extensive network of roads, totaling over 400,000 km, facilitating trade, military movement, and communication across the empire.

These facts underscore the diverse and profound contributions of ancient societies to the development of human civilization, many of which form the foundation of modern technologies and knowledge systems.

Continuing from the previous exploration into the innovations and mysteries of ancient societies, here are additional facts that further illustrate the ingenuity and breadth of ancient civilizations' contributions:

26. **The Silk Road**: Established during the Han Dynasty of China in the 2nd century BC, this network of trade routes connected East and West, facilitating not only commerce but also the exchange of culture, religion, and technology.

27. **Ancient Solar Observatories**: The Chankillo observatory in Peru, dating back to 300 BC, consists of thirteen towers that served as a solar calendar, accurately marking the solstices and equinoxes.

28. **The Great Zimbabwe:** Built in the 11th century, this African city-state demonstrates advanced architectural techniques, with structures made of precisely fitted stones without mor tar.

29. **Hellenistic Hydraulic Technology:** The Greeks developed the Archimedes Screw in the 3rd century BC, an innovative device for raising water, showing early fluid dynamics understanding.

30. **The Colosseum's Velarium:** The ancient Romans designed a massive retractable awning for the Colosseum, providing sun and rain protection for spectators, an early example of large-scale architectural engineering.

31. **Mohenjo-Daro**: This ancient Indus Valley Civilization city (2600–1900 BC) featured advanced urban planning, including a sophisticated drainage system and water supply, illustrating early sanitary engineering.

32. **The Damascus Steel**: Developed around 300–500 AD, this type of steel was used to make blades sharper, more resilient, and more flexible than any others of its time, showing advanced metallurgy.

33. **The Viking Sunstone:** Vikings possibly used a type of crystal called sunstone to navigate through foggy and cloudy conditions, a remarkable navigation aid before the magnetic compass became widespread in Europe.

34. **Olmec Colossal Heads**: Dating back to at least 900 BC, these massive stone sculptures reflect the Olmec civilization's artistic skill and organizational ability, given the resources required for their creation and transport.

35. **The Floating Gardens of Xochimilco:** The Aztecs developed chinampas, or floating gardens, for agriculture, an innovative solution to lack of arable land in the marshy areas of Lake Texcoco.

36. **The Heidelberg Tun**: Constructed in 1751, this giant wine barrel in Heidelberg Castle illustrates the advanced craftsmanship and engineering of the time, with a capacity of about 219,000 liters.

37. **The Lighthouse of Alexandria**: One of the Seven Wonders of the Ancient World, built around 280 BC, it stood as one of the tallest man-made structures for centuries, demonstrating advanced architectural and optical engineering.

38. **Ancient Clocks**: The ancient Egyptians developed the water clock, or clepsydra, around 1500 BC, one of the earliest timekeeping devices that allowed for the measurement of time at night.

39. **Mesopotamian Glass Making**: Around 3500 BC, Mesopotamians began manufacturing glass, leading to the development of glassblowing by the 1st century BC, a technology that drastically changed the production of glass vessels.

40. **The Stepwells of India**: Constructed as early as the 3rd century AD, stepwells are a unique form of water storage systems, illustrating ancient India's architectural and environmental ingenuity.

41. **The Etruscan Book of Gold**: Dating to the 6th century BC, this artifact demonstrates the Etruscans' advanced work in gold and their early use of writing, contributing significantly to our understanding of their culture.

42. **Ancient Roman Heating Systems**: The hypocaust, developed by the Romans, was an early central heating system used to heat houses and public baths, showcasing their advanced understanding of engineering and thermodynamics.

43. **The Tunnel of Eupalinos in Samos:** Constructed in the 6th century BC, this aqueduct tunnel is one of the earliest known examples of a tunnel dug from both ends that met in the middle, an incredible feat of engineering.

44. **The Calendar of Tlaloc**: This Aztec calendar, dating back to the 15th century, not only meticulously tracked time but also played a significant role in religious and agricultural practices, reflecting the integration of astronomy, mathematics, and religion.

45. **The Alhambra's Water System:** The sophisticated water system of the Alhambra in Granada, Spain, built in the 13th century, showcases the Islamic world's advanced knowledge in hydraulic engineering, providing water for baths, gardens, and fountains.

46. **The Mesoamerican Ballgame:** Originating around 1400 BC, this game was not only a sport but also held significant religious and social importance, demonstrating complex cultural practices.

47. **Ancient Tattooing:** Evidence suggests that tattooing was practiced by ancient cultures worldwide, including the Egyptians and Ötzi the Iceman, who lived around 3250 BC, indicating early forms of body art and personal expression.

48. **The Iron Pillar of Delhi**: Demonstrating sophisticated corrosion-resistant metallurgy, this pillar, dating back to the 4th century AD, remains largely rust-free after 1600 years.

49. **The Ancient City of Petra:** Built in the 4th century BC, Petra demonstrates the Nabataeans' advanced rock-cut architecture and water management system, including water conduits and cisterns.

50. **Göbekli Tepe**: Dating back to the 10th millennium BC, this archaeological site in Turkey contains the world's oldest known megaliths, suggesting early complex societal structures and possibly the first religious temple structure.

These facts further highlight the depth and diversity of ancient societies' innovations, many of which have laid foundational elements for various aspects of modern civilization, from architecture and engineering to social and religious practices.

Section 4.2: <u>Historical Coincidences</u>

The fabric of history is woven with surprising connections and events that reveal the interconnectedness of humanity across different eras and regions. These unexpected links often shed light on the complexities of historical developments, showing how ideas, inventions, and individuals have influenced the course of history in unforeseen ways. Here are facts that explore some of these fascinating historical connections and events:

1. **Tea and the American Revolution**: The taxation of tea, symbolized by the Boston Tea Party in 1773, played a pivotal role in escalating tensions that led to the American Revolution.

2. **The Library of Alexandria and the Spread of Knowledge**: The destruction of the Library of Alexandria, a significant loss of ancient knowledge, indirectly contributed to the dispersal of Greek scholars, spreading their knowledge throughout the Mediterranean and influencing the Islamic world and the Renaissance.

3. **The Black Death and the Renaissance:** The Black Death (1347-1351) devastated Europe's population but led to significant social, economic, and cultural shifts that contributed to the emergence of the Renaissance.

4. **Volcanic Eruptions and the French Revolution:** The 1783 Laki volcanic fissure eruption in Iceland caused widespread crop failures and economic hardship, contributing to the social unrest that led to the French Revolution.

5. **The Fall of Constantinople and the Age of Exploration:** The Ottoman Empire's conquest of Constantinople in 1453 cut off Europe's direct trade routes to Asia, spurring European explorations that eventually led to the discovery of the Americas.

6. **The Potato Famine and the Expansion of the United States:** The Irish Potato Famine in the mid-19th century led to a massive wave of Irish immigration to the United States, significantly influencing its urban populations and culture.

7. **The Treaty of Tordesillas and the Portuguese Language in Brazil**: The 1494 Treaty of Tordesillas, intended to resolve territorial disputes between Spain and Portugal, inadvertently set the stage for Portuguese to become the dominant language in Brazil.

8. **World War II and the Creation of the United Nations**: The devastation of World War II directly led to the establishment of the United Nations in 1945, with the goal of preventing future global conflicts.

9. **The Gutenberg Press and the Protestant Reformation**: The invention of the printing press by Johannes Gutenberg in the 15th century made books more accessible, facilitating the spread of Martin Luther's ideas and the Protestant Reformation.

10. **The Russo-Japanese War and the Russian Revolution:** Japan's victory in the Russo- Japanese War (1904-1905) highlighted the weakness of Tsarist Russia, contributing to the unrest that led to the 1905 Revolution and eventually the 1917 Russian Revolution.

11. **The Silk Road and the Spread of the Black Death:** The trade routes of the Silk Road facilitated the spread of the Black Death from Asia to Europe, illustrating the early globalization of disease.

12. **The Assassination of Archduke Franz Ferdinand and World War I:** This event in 1914 triggered a complex web of alliances and conflicts, leading to the outbreak of World War I.

13. **The Discovery of the Rosetta Stone and Egyptian Hieroglyphs**: The 1799 discovery of the Rosetta Stone made it possible to decipher Egyptian hieroglyphs, unlocking the history of ancient Egypt.

14. **The Suez Crisis and the Cold War:** The 1956 Suez Crisis marked a significant moment in the Cold War, highlighting the decline of British and French imperial power and the rise of American and Soviet influence in the Middle East.

15. **The Cuban Missile Crisis and the Nuclear Test Ban Treaty:** The near-miss of nuclear war during the Cuban Missile Crisis in 1962 led directly to the signing of the Partial Nuclear Test Ban Treaty in 1963.

16. **The Spanish Flu and the End of World War I**: The 1918 influenza pandemic hastened the end of World War I as countries, already devastated by war, struggled to cope with the additional burden of the pandemic.

17. **The Great Fire of London and Urban Planning**: The reconstruction of London following the Great Fire of 1666 led to significant changes in urban planning and building regulations.

18. **The Wright Brothers and the Space Age:** The Wright Brothers' first powered flight in 1903 set the stage for advances in aviation that would eventually lead to human spaceflight.

19. **The Fall of the Berlin Wall and the End of the Cold War**: The unexpected fall of the Berlin Wall in 1989 symbolized the end of the Cold War and led to the reunification of Germany.

20. **The Magna Carta and the U.S. Constitution**: The Magna Carta, signed in 1215, influenced the development of constitutional law and the creation of the U.S. Constitution.

21. **The Discovery of Penicillin and Modern Medicine:** Alexander Fleming's accidental discovery of penicillin in 1928 revolutionized medicine and the treatment of bacterial infections.

22. **The Columbian Exchange and Global Cuisine**: The exchange of crops and animals following Christopher Columbus's voyages had a profound impact on global cuisine, introducing new foods to different parts of the world.

23. **The California Gold Rush and the Transcontinental Railroad**: The influx of people to California during the Gold Rush in the mid-19th century accelerated the push for the construction of the Transcontinental Railroad.

24. **The Dinosaur Bone Wars and Paleontology:** The competitive fossil hunting by Edward Drinker Cope and Othniel Charles Marsh in the late 19th century significantly advanced the field of paleontology.

25. **The Invention of the Telegraph and the Decline of the Pony Express**: The success of the telegraph system in the mid-19th century rendered the Pony Express obsolete, showcasing the impact of technological innovation on communication methods.

.The interwoven threads of history often reveal unexpected connections and consequences, illustrating how events, cultures, and inventions across different periods and locations have shaped the world in unforeseen ways. Here are 25 more intriguing facts that explore these surprising links and historical outcomes:

26. **The Spice Trade and Global Exploration.** The lucrative spice trade in the Middle Ages spurred European explorations, leading to the discovery of new continents and the establishment of trade routes around Africa and across the Atlantic and Pacific Oceans.

27. **The French Encyclopédie and the Enlightenment**: The publication of the Encyclopédie in the 18th century, edited by Denis Diderot and Jean le Rond d'Alembert, played a pivotal role in spreading the ideas of the Enlightenment, challenging traditional ways of thinking about science, religion, and governance.

28. **The Industrial Revolution and Environmental Change**: The onset of the Industrial Revolution in the late 18th century marked a significant turning point in human history, leading to unprecedented economic growth but also environmental changes and social upheaval.

29. **The Bubonic Plague and Labor Movements**: The Black Death significantly reduced the population of Europe, leading to a scarcity of labor and strengthening the bargaining power of peasants and workers, indirectly contributing to the end of feudalism.

30. **The Construction of the Panama Canal and Global Trade**: Completed in 1914, the Panama Canal dramatically shortened maritime travel times between the Atlantic and Pacific Oceans, boosting global trade and military strategic mobility.

31. **The Atomic Bomb and the Cold War:** The development and use of atomic bombs at the end of World War II not only brought about the end of the conflict but also initiated the nuclear arms race, a central element of the Cold War.

32. **The Invention of the Printing Press and the Spread of Literacy**: Johannes Gutenberg's invention in the 15th century made books more affordable and accessible, leading to a rise in literacy rates and the spread of new ideas.

33. **The Salem Witch Trials and American Legal Reform**: The hysteria and injustices of the Salem witch trials in the late 17th century contributed to changes in American legal practices, emphasizing the importance of evidence and the right to legal representation.

34. **The Discovery of the New World and the Columbian Exchange:** Christopher Columbus's voyages to the Americas initiated the Columbian Exchange, which dramatically impacted the agriculture, cuisine, and demographics of both the Old World and the New World.

35. **The Fall of the Roman Empire and the Rise of the Byzantine Empire:** The decline of the Western Roman Empire led to the rise of the Byzantine Empire in the East, preserving Greek and Roman knowledge and culture through the Middle Ages.

36. **The American Civil War and Medical Advances:** The American Civil War spurred advancements in medical treatment and surgery, including the establishment of ambulance services and improvements in hospital care.

37. **The Invention of Air Conditioning and Population Growth in the American South**: The widespread adoption of air conditioning in the mid-20th century made the hot, humid climates of the American South more livable, contributing to significant population growth in the region.

38. **The Battle of Saratoga and French Involvement in the American Revolution**: The American victory at the Battle of Saratoga in 1777 was a turning point in the American Revolution, convincing France to enter the war on the side of the Americans.

39. **The Treaty of Versailles and World War II**: The harsh terms imposed on Germany by the Treaty of Versailles after World War I contributed to economic hardship and political instability, setting the stage for World War II.

40. **The Great Migration and the Harlem Renaissance**: The Great Migration of African Americans from the rural South to urban areas in the North contributed to the cultural explosion of the Harlem Renaissance in the 1920s.

41. **The Discovery of Oil in the Middle East and Global Politics:** The discovery and exploitation of oil reserves in the Middle East in the 20th century have had profound effects on global politics, economics, and environmental policies.

42. **The Irish Monks and the Preservation of Western Literature**: During the Dark Ages, Irish monks played a crucial role in preserving and copying classical and religious texts, contributing to the survival of Western literature and learning.

43. **The Assassination of Julius Caesar and the Rise of the Roman Empire:** The assassination of Julius Caesar in 44 BC led to a series of civil wars, ultimately resulting in the end of the Roman Republic and the rise of the Roman Empire under Augustus.

44. **The Defeat of the Spanish Armada and the Rise of the British Empire:** The defeat of the Spanish Armada by the English in 1588 marked the decline of Spanish naval dominance and the rise of Britain as a world naval power, paving the way for the British Empire.

45. **The Discovery of Insulin and Diabetes Treatment**: The discovery of insulin in the early 20th century by Frederick Banting and Charles Best represented a major breakthrough in the treatment of diabetes, saving countless lives.

46. **The Chornobyl Disaster and the End of the Soviet Union**: The Chornobyl nuclear disaster in 1986 exposed the shortcomings of the Soviet system, contributing to the growing discontent that led to the dissolution of the Soviet Union.

47. **The Invention of the Internet and the Information Age**: The development of the internet has revolutionized communication, commerce, and entertainment, marking the beginning of the Information Age.

48. **The Magna Carta and Modern Democracy**: The signing of the Magna Carta in 1215 laid the foundation for the development of constitutional law and modern democracy, emphasizing the principle that the king was subject to the law.

49. **The Sinking of the Titanic and Maritime Safety Regulations**: The tragic sinking of the Titanic in 1912 led to significant changes in maritime safety regulations, including the requirement for sufficient lifeboats for all passengers.

50. **The End of the Cold War and the Expansion of the European Union**: The end of the Cold War removed political barriers in Europe, facilitating the expansion of the European Union and the integration of Eastern European countries.

These facts highlight the intricate web of causes and effects that have shaped historical developments, revealing the unexpected ways in which events, technologies, and ideas have interlinked to influence the global narrative.

Section 4.3: Lost Treasures and Artifacts

Sure, crafting a list of facts about the discovery and loss of significant historical items involves exploring a vast range of artifacts, treasures, and relics that hold immense cultural, historical, and monetary value. These stories span across continents and eras, encompassing ancient civilizations, maritime discoveries, wartime loots, and modern-day archeological finds. Let's dive into some fascinating facts:

1. **The Rosetta Stone's Discovery (1799)**: Found by French soldiers near the town of Rosetta in Egypt, this granodiorite stele was the key to deciphering Egyptian hieroglyphs, significantly advancing our understanding of ancient Egyptian civilization.

2. **Loss and Recovery of the Mona Lisa (1911):** Leonardo da Vinci's Mona Lisa was stolen from the Louvre in 1911 by an Italian handyman, Vincenzo Peruggia, only to be recovered two years later in Italy.

3. **The Dead Sea Scrolls (1947):** Discovered in a series of caves near the Dead Sea, these texts include the earliest known surviving copies of biblical and extra-biblical documents, shedding light on Judaism and the origins of Christianity.

4. **Sutton Hoo Ship Burial (1939):** Unearthed in Suffolk, England, this early medieval graveyard contained a ship burial filled with artifacts of outstanding art-historical and archaeological significance, illuminating the Anglo-Saxon period.

5. **The Terracotta Army Discovery (1974):** Farmers digging a well near Xi'an, China, stumbled upon one of the most significant archaeological finds: a vast army of life-size terracotta soldiers guarding the tomb of China's first emperor, Qin Shi Huang.

6. **The Titanic Wreckage (1985):** The RMS Titanic was found split in two at the bottom of the North Atlantic Ocean, over 70 years after it sank on its maiden voyage, revealing new details about the infamous maritime disaster.

7. **The Theft of The Scream (1994):** Edvard Munch's iconic painting was stolen from the National Gallery in Oslo, Norway, but fortunately recovered later that year in a sting operation.

8. **Discovery of Machu Picchu (1911):** The lost city of the Incas was brought to international attention by Hiram Bingham, who was led there by local farmers, revealing one of the most intact and impressive ancient sites in the world.

9. **The Amber Room (Disappeared 1945):** Considered the "Eighth Wonder of the World," this ornate chamber decorated in amber panels backed with gold leaf and mirrors was looted by Nazi Germany and has been missing since the end of World War II.

10. **Cleopatra's Tomb (Undiscovered):** Despite being one of the most famous figures in ancient history, the final resting place of Cleopatra remains one of Egyptology's greatest mysteries.

11. **The Honjo Masamune (Lost Post-WWII):** A symbol of the Shogunate during the Edo period in Japan, this masterfully crafted sword disappeared after WWII during the American occupa tion.

12. **The Discovery of King Tutankhamun's Tomb (1922):** Howard Carter's discovery of King Tut's nearly intact tomb in the Valley of the Kings was one of the most significant archaeological finds, providing a wealth of artifacts and insight into ancient Egyptian burial practices.

13. **The Benin Bronzes (1897):** These cultural artifacts were looted from the Kingdom of Benin (now Nigeria) by the British and are currently the subject of international repatriation effor ts.

14. **The Loss of the Imperial Regalia of Japan (Lost 1185):** According to legend, the sacred treasures were lost at sea during the Battle of Dan-no-ura, a major battle of the Genpei War.

15. **The Cuerdale Hoard (1840):** One of the largest hoards of Viking silver ever found, discovered by workmen in Lancashire, England, it consists of over 8,600 items, including silver coins, jewelry, and ingots.

16. **The San José Galleon (Discovered 2015):** Sunk in 1708 near the coast of Colombia, the Spanish galleon was laden with gold, silver, and emeralds worth billions today. Its discovery has been mired in legal battles over ownership.

17. **The Gospel of Judas (Rediscovered 1970s, Published 2006):** This ancient text, thought to have been destroyed, offers a different perspective on the relationship between Jesus Christ and Judas Iscariot, challenging traditional narratives of Christianity.

18. **The Isabella Stewart Gardner Museum Heist (1990):** In the largest art theft in history, 13 works valued at over $500 million were stolen from this Boston museum and have yet to be recovered.

19. **The Antikythera Mechanism Discovery (1901):** An ancient Greek analog computer used to predict astronomical positions and eclipses for calendrical and astrological purposes, it was found in a shipwreck off the coast of the Greek island Antikythera.

20. **The Nefertiti Bust Discovery (1912):** Found in the ruins of Amarna, Egypt, the painted stucco-coated limestone bust of Queen Nefertiti has become one of the most copied works of ancient Egypt.

21. **The Baghdad Battery (1938):** These terracotta pots, dating back to the Parthian period, are believed by some to be among the earliest forms of batteries, suggesting advanced knowledge of electricity among ancient peoples.

22. **The Theft of The Just Judges (1934):** Part of the Ghent Altarpiece painted by Jan van Eyck, this panel was stolen from Saint Bavo's Cathedral in Ghent, Belgium, and remains missing to this day.

23. **Discovery of the HMS Erebus (2014.** One of the two ships of Sir John Franklin's ill-fated Arctic expedition of 1845, its discovery has shed light on the final days of the expedition's attempt to chart the Northwest Passage.

24. **The Cheapside Hoard (1912)**: Discovered in an old wooden casket beneath London's Cheapside Street, this collection of late 16th and early 17th-century jewelry is the largest known cache of Elizabethan and Jacobean jewelry.

25. **The Disappearance of the Amber Room (1941):** Crafted entirely of amber panels, gold leaf, and mirrors, this masterpiece was stolen by Nazi Germany during World War II and has never been recovered.

These facts illustrate not only the wealth of our shared global heritage but also the ongoing challenges of preservation, recovery, and ethical stewardship of cultural artifacts.

26. **Viking Settlement Discovery in Newfoundland (1960):** Evidence of Norse presence in North America was confirmed with the discovery of a Viking settlement at L'Anse aux Meadows, predating Columbus's voyages by centuries.

27. **Theft of the Irish Crown Jewels (1907):** The jewels were stolen from Dublin Castle and have never been recovered, remaining one of Ireland's most infamous mysteries.

28. **Discovery of Ötzi the Iceman (1991):** Found in the Alps on the border between Austria and Italy, this well-preserved natural mummy of a man who lived around 3400 BCE has provided invaluable insights into Copper Age Europe.

29. **The Peking Man Fossils Loss (1941):** A collection of Homo erectus fossils discovered near Beijing in the early 20th century disappeared during WWII while being transported for

safekeeping.

30. **The Raft of the Medusa Real-Life Event and Painting (1816-1819):** The French frigate Méduse ran aground off the coast of Mauritania, leading to a harrowing tale of survival. Théodore Géricault's painting dramatically captures this event, highlighting the disaster's impact on French society.

31. **The Discovery of Pompeii (1748):** The ancient Roman city was buried under volcanic ash and pumice in the eruption of Mount Vesuvius in 79 CE. Its excavation provided an extraordinarily detailed insight into the life of a city at the height of the Roman Empire.

32. **The Theft of a Van Gogh Painting (2020):** Vincent van Gogh's painting "Spring Garden" was stolen from a museum in The Netherlands during an overnight raid, illustrating the ongoing threat to valuable artworks.

33. **Discovery of the Higgs Boson Particle (2012):** Although not a physical object, the discovery of the Higgs boson at CERN's Large Hadron Collider marked a significant milestone in understanding the fundamental structure of the universe.

34. **The Blackbeard's Queen Anne's Revenge Shipwreck Discovery (1996):** The infamous pirate Blackbeard's flagship was discovered off the coast of North Carolina, providing historical artifacts and insights into early 18th-century piracy.

35. **The Sappho Manuscript Discoveries:** Fragments of works by the ancient Greek poet Sappho have been discovered intermittently, most significantly in the 19th and 20th centuries, expanding our understanding of her poetry and life in ancient Lesbos.

36. **The Disappearance of the Fabergé Eggs (Post-1917):** Of the 50 Imperial eggs crafted by Carl Fabergé for the Russian Imperial family, several are unaccounted for following the Russian Revolution, leading to ongoing searches and high-profile rediscoveries.

37. **The Lascaux Cave Paintings Discovery (1940):** Found by teenagers in France, these Paleolithic cave paintings are estimated to be up to 20,000 years old, offering profound insights into early human creativity and spirituality.

38. **Loss of the Musashi Battleship (1944):** The Japanese Navy's Musashi, one of the largest and most heavily armed battleships ever constructed, was sunk during WWII and discovered in 2015 in the Sibuyan Sea in the Philippines.

39. **Discovery of the RMS Republic's Wreckage (1981):** Sunk in 1909 after a collision, the RMS Republic was rumored to carry a vast treasure. Its discovery has sparked interest but the treasure remains elusive.

40. **The Gurlitt Trove (Discovered 2012):** Over 1,400 artworks, including pieces by Picasso and Matisse, were discovered in the apartment of Cornelius Gurlitt in Munich, many of which were suspected to have been looted by the Nazis.

41. **The Bactrian Gold (Discovered 1978):** A collection of over 20,000 gold ornaments from the ancient Bactrian civilization was found in Afghanistan, miraculously surviving the turmoil of subsequent decades.

42. **Discovery of the Voynich Manuscript (1912):** This illustrated codex is written in an unknown writing system, dating back to the 15th century. Its purpose and the meaning of its text remain a mystery.

43. **The Theft of the Codex Calixtinus (2011):** This 12th-century illuminated manuscript, a jewel of medieval literature, was stolen from the Cathedral of Santiago de Compostela in Spain but fortunately recovered in 2012.

44. **Discovery of the Clotilda (2019):** The last known ship to bring enslaved Africans to the United States was discovered in the Mobile River in Alabama, providing a direct link to America's history of slavery.

45. **The Destruction of Palmyra (2015):** This ancient Syrian city, a UNESCO World Heritage Site, suffered significant damage at the hands of ISIS, including the destruction of the Temple of Bel, a loss to both history and world culture.

46. **The Caesarea Sunken Treasure (2015):** Over 2,000 gold coins from the Fatimid Caliphate were discovered by divers in the ancient harbor of Caesarea, Israel, marking the largest find of gold coins ever discovered in Israel.

47. **The Return of the Elgin Marbles Debate:** These Parthenon marbles, taken from Greece to Britain in the early 19th century, have been the subject of an ongoing debate regarding their repatriation to Greece.

48. **The Recovery of the Apollo 11 Engines (2013):** Amazon CEO Jeff Bezos funded an expedition that successfully recovered engines from the Apollo 11 mission from the Atlantic Ocean, highlighting the importance of preserving space exploration history.

49. **The Disappearance of the World Trade Center's Cortlandt Street Mosaic (2001):** This artwork was destroyed in the 9/11 attacks, representing a cultural loss amidst the tragic events of that day.

50. **The Recovery of the Atocha Treasure (1985):** The shipwreck of the Spanish galleon Nuestra Señora de Atocha was discovered off the coast of Florida, yielding an enormous cache of silver, gold, and emeralds from the 17th century.

These facts further demonstrate the breadth of humanity's endeavors, achievements, and occasionally, our follies and tragedies, capturing the essence of our quest to understand and preserve our shared heritage.

Chapter 5: Cultural Curiosities

Section 5.1: Unusual Traditions Worldwide

Exploring unique cultural practices and festivals around the world opens a fascinating window into the diversity and creativity of human societies. From ancient rituals to modern-day celebrations, these events offer insights into the values, traditions, and communal life of people across the globe. Here are intriguing facts about various cultural practices and festivals:

1. **La Tomatina (Spain)**: Held annually in Buñol, participants throw thousands of overripe tomatoes at each other in a vibrant, red-soaked spectacle that celebrates community and fun.

2. **The Day of the Dead (Mexico):** A UNESCO Intangible Cultural Heritage, this festival blends Indigenous Aztec rituals with Catholicism, where families honor deceased loved ones with altars and offerings.

3. **Holi (India):** Known as the Festival of Colors, Holi celebrates the arrival of spring with people throwing colored powder and water at each other, symbolizing the victory of good over evil.

4. **Yi Peng Lantern Festival (Thailand):** Part of the Loy Krathong celebrations, thousands of lanterns are released into the night sky, symbolizing the letting go of misfortunes and bad luck.

5. **Burning Man (USA):** An annual gathering in the Nevada desert that emphasizes art, self- expression, and community, culminating in the burning of a large wooden effigy.

6. **Carnival (Brazil):** The pre-Lenten festival is famed for its extravagant parades featuring samba dancers in colorful costumes, reflecting a mix of African, Portuguese, and Indigenous cultures.

7. **Midsummer (Sweden):** Celebrated during the summer solstice, festivities include dancing around the maypole, singing traditional songs, and enjoying a feast that includes herring and new potatoes.

8. **Diwali (India and Worldwide):** The Hindu Festival of Lights, Diwali, signifies the victory of light over darkness with millions of lamps lit at homes, temples, and public spaces.

9. **Mardi Gras (USA):** Known especially in New Orleans, Mardi Gras marks a time of merry-making and parading before the somber season of Lent, with roots tracing back to French Catholic traditions.

10. **Oktoberfest (Germany):** Originating in Munich, it's the world's largest Volksfest combining a massive beer festival with a traveling funfair. The event celebrates Bavarian culture, especially its iconic beer and cuisine.

11. **The Running of the Bulls (Spain):** Part of the San Fermín festival in Pamplona, this event involves running in front of a group of bulls as they charge through the city's streets.

12. **Cheung Chau Bun Festival (Hong Kong):** This festival features a parade with children dressed as deities floating above the crowd, and a competition to climb a tower covered in buns.

13. **Up Helly Aa (Scotland):** Europe's largest fire festival, celebrating Viking heritage in the Shetland Islands with torch-lit processions and the burning of a Viking longship.

14. **Songkran Water Festival (Thailand):** Marks the Thai New Year with the throwing of water, symbolizing washing away bad luck and misfortunes.

15. **Pushkar Camel Fair (India):** One of India's largest camel, horse, and livestock fairs, also featuring competitions, folk music, and dance, highlighting Rajasthani culture.

16. **Gion Matsuri (Japan):** A month-long festival in Kyoto featuring processions of massive floats, traditional music, and performances, rooted in purification rituals to appease the gods.

17. **Krampusnacht (Austria and Germany):** Celebrated on the eve of St. Nicholas Day, Krampusnacht features parades of Krampus, a horned anthropomorphic figure who punishes naughty children.

18. **The Edinburgh Festival Fringe (Scotland):** The world's largest arts festival, where performers take to hundreds of stages all over the city to present shows for every taste.

19. **The Battle of the Oranges (Italy):** Held in Ivrea, this festival includes a community-wide orange-throwing battle that commemorates the city's defiance against tyranny.

20. **White Nights Festival (Russia)**: Celebrated during the season of the midnight sun, with ballet, opera, and classical music performances, culminating in the Scarlet Sails celebration in St. Petersburg.

21. **Timkat (Ethiopia):** An Ethiopian Orthodox celebration marking the baptism of Jesus in the River Jordan, featuring processions, music, dancing, and the ritual reenactment of baptism.

22. **Inti Raymi (Peru):** A traditional Inca festival that takes place in Cusco, celebrating the sun god Inti, featuring processions, dances, and sacrifices to ensure a good harvest.

23. **The Regatta of the Ancient Maritime Republics (Italy):** A historical boat race between Amalfi, Genoa, Pisa, and Venice, celebrating the maritime prowess and heritage of these former maritime republics.

24. **Maslenitsa (Russia):** Also known as Pancake Week, this Slavic festival marks the end of winter with the consumption of pancakes and culminates in the burning of a straw effigy.

25. **Kumbh Mela (India):** Held every twelve years in four rotating locations, it's one of the world's largest religious gatherings, where Hindus bathe in a sacred river to cleanse sins and achieve moksha.

These facts highlight the incredible diversity of cultural practices and festivals around the world, each with its unique significance and way of bringing communities together.

Delving further into the rich tapestry of global cultures reveals even more unique practices and festivals, each with its own story and significance. Here are 25 additional fascinating cultural facts:

26. **Feria de Las Flores (Colombia):** Held in Medellín, the Festival of Flowers is a celebration of Colombia's flower-growing tradition, featuring flower parades, live music, and Ballesteros (flower vendors) carrying elaborate floral arrangements.

27. **Sky Lantern Festival (Taiwan):** Also known as Pingxi Lantern Festival, where thousands of sky lanterns are released into the night sky with wishes written on them, creating a breathtaking spectacle.

28. **Glastonbury Festival (UK):** One of the biggest music and performing arts festivals in the world, held in Somerset, celebrating contemporary music, dance, and art.

29. **Cherry Blossom Festival (Japan)**: Known as Hanami, this festival celebrates the fleeting beauty of cherry blossoms, with people gathering in parks for picnics under the blooming trees.

30. **Harbin International Ice and Snow Sculpture Festival (China):** The largest ice and snow festival in the world, showcasing massive ice sculptures and buildings constructed from blocks of ice taken from the Songhua River.

31. **Ganesh Chaturthi (India):** A Hindu festival celebrating the birth of Lord Ganesha, known for grand idols of Ganesha that are worshipped and then immersed in water bodies.

32. **Il Palio di Siena (Italy):** A historic horse race that takes place in Siena's Piazza del Campo, where the city's districts compete fiercely for pride and glory.

33. **Naadam Festival (Mongolia):** A traditional festival in Mongolia showcasing the "Three Games of Men": wrestling, horse racing, and archery, rooted in nomadic culture.

34. **Vivid Sydney (Australia):** An annual festival of light, music, and ideas, featuring outdoor lighting sculptures and installations, along with cutting-edge contemporary music.

35. **Mevlana Whirling Dervishes Festival (Turkey):** Celebrates the life and teachings of the Sufi mystic Rumi, with participants performing the Sema ceremony, a spiritual dance.

36. **Cascamorras (Spain):** Participants from two towns, Guadix and Baza, attempt to claim a statue of the Virgin Mary by racing to the opposing town and back, all while being covered in black grease or paint.

37. **Wife Carrying Championship (Finland):** An annual event in Sonkajärvi, where competitors race while carrying their wives or female partners on their backs through an obstacle course.

38. **La Fête de Marquette (Madagascar):** A festival celebrating Marquette's French heritage with live music, food, and cultural activities, showcasing the island's unique blend of African and French influences.

39. **Junkanoo (Bahamas):** A traditional street parade of music, dance, and art held in Nassau (and other towns) during Boxing Day and New Year's Day, featuring elaborate costumes and energetic performances.

40. **The Calcio Storico (Italy):** An ancient form of football from the 16th century, played in Florence with traditional rules and costumes, combining elements of soccer, rugby, and wrestling.

41. **The Albuquerque International Balloon Fiesta (USA):** The largest hot air balloon festival in the world, featuring over 500 balloons, attracting pilots and spectators from around the globe.

42. **Papua New Guinea Cultural Show (Papua New Guinea)**: Showcases the diverse cultures of Papua New Guinea, including traditional dance, music, and dress, representing hundreds of tribal groups.

43. **Festival au Desert (Mali):** Inspired by traditional Tuareg festivals, this music event near Timbuktu features performances by Malian and international artists, celebrating peace, tolerance, and cultural exchange.

44. **Midsommar (Sweden):** A celebration of the summer solstice, where Swedes enjoy the longest day of the year with maypole dancing, flower wreaths, and traditional songs and games.

45. **Kings Day (Netherlands):** Celebrated on April 27th, marking the birth of King Willem-Alexander, with street parties, flea markets, and everyone wearing orange, the national color.

46. **The Isle of Man TT (UK)**: A motorcycle racing event held annually on the Isle of Man since 1907, famous for its challenging course and being one of the oldest continuous motorsport events in the world.

47. **Rath Yatra (India):** A Hindu festival associated with Lord Jagannath held at Puri in the state of Odisha, famous for the chariot procession in which the deities are pulled on huge, elaborately decorated chariots.

48. **Descent of the Gualí River (Colombia):** An annual event in Honda where locals navigate the river on rafts made of guadua bamboo, celebrating the region's river culture and history.

49. **Hogmanay (Scotland):** The Scottish celebration of the New Year, marked by street parties, traditional music, and the famous Edinburgh Hogmanay fireworks display.

50. **Lantern Festival (China)**: Marks the end of Chinese New Year celebrations, with lantern displays, lion and dragon dances, and the eating of tangyuan (sweet rice balls), symbolizing family reunion and societal harmony.

Section 5.2: Language and Literature Oddities

The evolution of language and the written word is a captivating journey through human history, marking significant milestones in our intellectual, cultural, and social development. Here are fascinating facts about this evolution:

1. **Origins of Language:** The exact origins of human language are unknown, but evidence suggests it could have developed between 50,000 and 150,000 years ago, coinciding with the emergence of behaviorally modern humans.

2. **First Writing System:** The earliest known writing system is cuneiform, developed by the Sumerians of Mesopotamia around 3400 BCE for accounting purposes, evolving from pictographs to cuneiform symbols.

3. **The Rosetta Stone:** Discovered in 1799, the Rosetta Stone was key to deciphering Egyptian hieroglyphs, thanks to its inscriptions in three scripts: hieroglyphic, demotic, and Greek.

4. **Phoenician Alphabet:** Around 1050 BCE, the Phoenicians developed an alphabet that greatly influenced the world; it was the precursor to Greek and Latin alphabets, among others.

5. **Invention of Paper:** Paper was invented in China by Cai Lun in the Han Dynasty around 105 CE, revolutionizing the way information was recorded and disseminated.

6. **Illuminated Manuscripts:** In the Middle Ages, European monasteries produced illuminated manuscripts, and beautifully decorated texts of religious and philosophical works, showcasing the artistry in written records.

7. **The Gutenberg Bible:** Johann Gutenberg's invention of the movable type printing press in 15th-century Europe revolutionized the production of books, making them more accessible and leading to increased literacy rates.

8. **First Dictionary:** The first known dictionary was compiled in Akkadian, a Semitic language, around the 8th century BCE. Samuel Johnson's "A Dictionary of the English Language" (1755) significantly influenced English dictionaries.

9. **Origin of Emojis:** Emojis, a modern form of communication, trace back to the first emoticon, :-) , created in 1982 by computer scientist Scott Fahlman to distinguish serious posts from jokes on a bulletin board system.

10. **The Sanskrit Connection:** Sanskrit, an ancient Indo-European language, has influenced many modern languages, demonstrating the interconnectedness of linguistic evolution.

11. **Logograms to Alphabets:** Writing systems evolved from logograms, symbols representing words or phrases, to alphabets representing sounds, enabling the transcription of a wide range of languages with relatively few symbols.

12. **Vulgar Latin to Romance Languages**: The transformation of Vulgar Latin, spoken by soldiers and settlers of the Roman Empire, into the Romance languages (Spanish, French, Italian, Portuguese, and Romanian) is a key example of language evolution.

13. **The Voynich Manuscript**: An undeciphered manuscript dating to the 15th century, written in an unknown script with elaborate illustrations, remains one of the most mysterious documents in the world of linguistics.

14. **Braille System:** Invented by Louis Braille in the 19th century, the Braille system of raised dots enables blind people to read and write, demonstrating the adaptability of written communica tion.

15. **Pidgins and Creoles:** Pidgins, simplified languages that develop as means of communication between groups not sharing a common language, can evolve into creoles, stable natural languages with native speakers.

16. **Oldest Known Alphabet:** The Proto-Sinaitic script, dating back to around 1800 BCE, is considered the earliest known alphabetic writing system, derived from Egyptian hieroglyphs.

17. **Spread of the Arabic Script:** The spread of Islam significantly contributed to the spread of the Arabic script, now used to write numerous languages including Persian, Urdu, and Malay.

18. **Linguistic Relativity:** The Sapir-Whorf hypothesis suggests that the structure of a language influences its speakers' worldview and cognition, highlighting the profound impact of language on human thought.

19. **Global Language Extinction:** Linguists estimate that, of the approximately 7,000 languages spoken today, half could disappear by the end of the century, highlighting the importance of preservation efforts.

20. **The First Printed Book:** The Diamond Sutra, a Buddhist text printed in 868 CE in China, is considered the world's oldest known printed book.

21. **Internet and Language Evolution:** The Internet has accelerated language evolution, creating a dynamic space for the rapid development of slang, jargon, and new forms of written expression like memes and tweets.

22. **Ogham:** An early medieval alphabet found primarily in Ireland and parts of Wales, Scotland, and England, Ogham consists of marks made on stone monuments and is one of the earliest forms of writing in the British Isles.

23. **Etruscan Language:** The Etruscan language, used in ancient Italy, remains only partially understood, illustrating the challenges in deciphering lost languages.

24. **Development of Esperanto:** In 1887, L. L. Zamenhof created Esperanto, an artificial language aimed at fostering international understanding, demonstrating attempts to transcend linguistic barriers.

25. **Influence of English:** English has become a global lingua franca, significantly influencing other languages and serving as a primary language in international communication, science, and technology.

These facts underscore the complexity and fluidity of language evolution, reflecting changes in human societies, technologies, and interactions throughout history.

.

Continuing the exploration of the fascinating evolution of language and the written word, here are 25 additional facts that delve deeper into the development, diversity, and dynamics of linguistic phenomena:

26. **Cave Paintings as Early Communication:** Prehistoric cave paintings, such as those found in Lascaux, France, dating back around 17,000 years, are believed to be among the earliest forms of communication, predating written language.

27. **Sogdian Alphabet Influence:** The Sogdian alphabet, used by the Sogdian traders who traveled the Silk Road, influenced the development of the Uyghur and Mongolian scripts, demonstrating the role of trade in language evolution.

28. **Linear B Decipherment:** In 1952, Michael Ventris deciphered Linear B, an ancient Mycenaean Greek script used for administrative and commercial transactions, revealing insights into early Greek civilization.

29. **Epic of Gilgamesh:** One of the earliest known works of literary writing, the Epic of Gilgamesh was written in Akkadian on clay tablets around the 18th century BCE.

30. **Tamil - One of the Oldest Living Languages:** Tamil, spoken in parts of India, Sri Lanka, and Singapore, is over 2,000 years old and is considered one of the oldest living languages in the world.

31. **The Codex Sinaiticus**: Dating back to the 4th century, the Codex Sinaiticus is one of the oldest and most complete manuscripts of the Bible, written in Greek.

32. **The Spread of the Cyrillic Alphabet:** Developed in the First Bulgarian Empire in the 9th century, the Cyrillic alphabet was created by Saints Cyril and Methodius to translate the Bible and other texts into the Slavic languages.

33. **Chinese Characters:** One of the oldest continuously used systems of writing in the world, Chinese characters have been in use for over 3,000 years, evolving from pictographs to the complex script used today.

34. **Maya Script Decipherment:** The Maya script, a sophisticated hieroglyphic system used in Mesoamerica, has been partially deciphered, revealing much about Mayan civilization, history, and culture.

35. **Zulu Click Languages:** The Zulu language, along with other Bantu languages, incorporates click sounds as consonants, showcasing the phonetic diversity of human languages.

36. **First Grammatical Descriptions:** The first known grammatical description was written by the Indian linguist Panini in the 4th century BCE, detailing Sanskrit grammar in his work "Ashtadhyayi."

37. **The Book of Kells:** Created around 800 CE, the Book of Kells is an illuminated manuscript of the Gospels in Latin, renowned for its exquisite artwork and calligraphy, showcasing early Christian art in Ireland.

38. **Hebrew's Revival:** Once primarily a liturgical language, Modern Hebrew was revived in the late 19th and early 20th centuries as a spoken and written language, becoming one of the official languages of Israel.

39. **Printing Press in East Asia:** Before Gutenberg's press, movable type printing technology was developed in East Asia. Bi Sheng in China invented ceramic movable type around 1040 CE.

40. **The Cherokee Syllabary:** In the 1820s, Sequoyah, a Cherokee silversmith, created a syllabary for the Cherokee language, significantly boosting literacy among the Cherokee people.

41. **Basque Language Mystery:** The Basque language (Euskara), spoken in the Basque Country in Spain and France, is a linguistic isolate, unrelated to any other language in Europe or the world, highlighting the diversity of human languages.

42. **Aksumite Script for Ge'ez:** The ancient kingdom of Aksum (modern-day Ethiopia and Eritrea) developed the Ge'ez script, which is still used today in the liturgical languages of the Ethiopian and Eritrean Orthodox Churches.

43. **The Gutenberg Galaxy:** Marshall McLuhan's concept of the "Gutenberg Galaxy" describes how the invention of the printing press and the printed book significantly transformed human consciousness and societal structures.

44. **Rongorongo of Easter Island:** The Rongorongo script of Easter Island is one of the few ancient scripts that remain undeciphered, posing significant questions about its origins and meanings.

45. **Armenian Alphabet Creation:** The Armenian alphabet was created by Mesrop Mashtots in 405 CE, enabling the preservation and dissemination of Armenian literature and culture.

46. **Indus Valley Script:** The Indus Valley Civilization (c. 3300–1300 BCE) developed a script that remains undeciphered, leaving a significant gap in our understanding of this ancient civilization.

47. **First Known Author:** Enheduanna, an Akkadian princess who lived around 2300 BCE, is often considered the world's first known author by name, with her works dedicated to the goddess Inanna.

48. **J.R.R. Tolkien's Constructed Languages:** Renowned author J.R.R. Tolkien created several languages for the people in his fictional world, demonstrating the depth of language construction for literary purposes.

49. **International Phonetic Alphabet (IPA):** Developed in the 19th century, the IPA is a system of phonetic notation designed to represent all the sounds of spoken languages, facilitating the study of linguistics and phonetics.

50. **Global Digital Communication:** The advent of the internet and digital communication has led to the rapid spread of English as a global lingua franca, while also fostering the preservation and revival of endangered languages through online communities.

These facts highlight the complexity and beauty of human communication, showcasing the innovative ways in which languages and scripts have evolved, adapted, and influenced each other across history and geography.

Section 5.3: Culinary Wonders

The culinary world is as diverse as it is fascinating, with each culture offering dishes that are unique and sometimes astonishing to outsiders. From ancient recipes born out of necessity to modern creations that push the boundaries of gastronomy, here are facts about some of the world's most unusual dishes and their origins:

1. **Hákarl (Iceland):** This traditional Icelandic dish consists of fermented shark meat. Originally developed by Vikings, the fermentation process makes the otherwise poisonous shark meat safe to eat.

2. **Casu Marzu (Italy):** A Sardinian cheese that means "rotten cheese," casu marzu is made by allowing flies to lay eggs in Pecorino cheese; the larvae ferment the cheese by breaking down its fats.

3. **Balut (Philippines):** A street food delicacy, balut is a fertilized duck egg with a partially developed embryo inside, boiled and eaten in the shell. It's believed to be an aphrodisiac and a high-protein snack.

4. **Surströmming (Sweden):** This is fermented Baltic sea herring, known for its strong smell. It's traditionally eaten with Swedish flatbread and potatoes. The fermentation process was originally a way to preserve fish.

5. **Century Eggs (China):** Also known as thousand-year eggs, these are preserved eggs that take several weeks to months to prepare by curing them in a mixture of clay, ash, salt, quicklime, and rice hulls.

6. **Fugu (Japan):** A delicacy made from the poisonous pufferfish. Chefs must undergo years of training to learn how to remove the toxic parts safely. Eating fugu was a status symbol among the samurai.

7. **Witchetty Grub (Australia):** Considered a bushfood delicacy among Indigenous Australians, witchetty grubs are large, white, wood-eating larvae of several moth species, rich in protein.

8. **Fried Tarantulas (Cambodia):** Originating from the town of Skuon, these crispy treats were first eaten by Cambodians during the food shortages under the Khmer Rouge regime.

9. **Stinkheads (Alaska):** Traditional Alaskan Inuit food, stinkheads are fermented fish heads, typically from salmon. They are buried in the ground in fermentation pits, then dug up and eaten after a few weeks.

10. **Escamoles (Mexico):** Known as "insect caviar," escamoles are the edible larvae and pupae of ants, harvested from the roots of agave plants. They are a delicacy dating back to the Aztecs.

11. **Lutefisk (Norway):** Dried whitefish, usually cod, prepared with lye. The lye softens the fish, which is then rehydrated by soaking in water before cooking. Lutefisk's origins trace back to the Vikings.

12. **Kopi Luwak (Indonesia):** The world's most expensive coffee, made from beans that have been eaten and excreted by the Asian palm civet. The fermentation process in the civet's intestines is said to give the coffee a unique flavor.

13. **Bird's Nest Soup (China):** Made from the nests of the swiftlet bird, which are built from solidified saliva. The nests are harvested from cave walls and dissolved in water to create a gelatinous soup.

14. **Haggis (Scotland):** A savory pudding containing sheep's heart, liver, and lungs, minced with onion, oatmeal, suet, spices, and salt, mixed with stock, and traditionally encased in the animal's stomach.

15. **Rocky Mountain Oysters (USA):** A dish made from the testicles of bulls, pigs, or sheep. The organs are often deep-fried and served as appetizers. The dish originated from ranching regions in the American West.

16. **Sannakji (South Korea):** A dish of live octopus, served still wriggling on the plate. It's cut into small pieces and seasoned with sesame oil and seeds. Eating it is a challenge due to the suction cups.

17. **Fried Brain Sandwiches (USA):** Once common in the central United States, this dish is made from sliced calves' brains, breaded and fried. It traces back to the region's German immigrant population.

18. **Durian (Southeast Asia):** Known as the "king of fruits," durian is famous for its strong odor, which some people find unbearable. Its creamy texture and sweet taste, however, are highly prized.

19. **Guinea Pig (Ecuador, Peru):** Known as "cuy," guinea pig is a traditional Andean dish. It's usually roasted whole and served with potatoes and corn. The practice dates back to pre-Columbian times.

20. **Snake Wine (Southeast Asia):** A beverage produced by infusing whole snakes in rice wine or grain alcohol. The drink is believed to have restorative properties according to traditional Chinese medicine.

21. **Jellied Moose Nose (Canada):** A traditional dish of Northern Canada, it involves boiling the nose of a moose with onions and spices, then slicing it and serving it cold in its congealed broth.

22. **Muktuk (Greenland, Northern Canada):** A traditional Inuit dish made from the skin and blubber of the bowhead whale, narwhal, or beluga. It is rich in vitamins and eaten raw, pickled, or frozen.

23. **Ant Egg Soup (Laos):** A seasonal delicacy, this soup is made with ant eggs and larvae collected from mango trees. It's a tangy and creamy soup, often compared to shrimp bisque.

24. **Boshintang (South Korea):** A controversial dish, this dog meat soup is believed to increase stamina and health. Its consumption dates back centuries but is now declining and controversial.

25. **Tuna Eyeballs (Japan):** Found in Japanese supermarkets and restaurants, tuna eyeballs are boiled or steamed and seasoned. They're considered a delicacy, with a taste similar to squid or octopus.

These dishes highlight the incredible diversity of global cuisines and the human ability to adapt to and make use of available resources. Whether born from necessity, tradition, or culinary experimentation, each dish tells a story of cultural identity and evolution.

The exploration of unusual dishes and food origins unveils the endless creativity and adaptability of human culinary practices. Here are more facts about some of the world's most intriguing and unique foods:

26. **Chapulines (Mexico):** Grasshoppers that have been toasted and flavored with garlic, lime, and salt or chili. This snack dates back to the Aztecs and is a sustainable protein source.

27. **Mopane Worms (Southern Africa):** Caterpillars of the Emperor Moth, dried or smoked, are a high-protein snack. They are an important source of nutrition in rural areas and are named after the mopane tree they feed on.

28. **Black Ivory Coffee (Thailand):** Similar to Kopi Luwak, this rare coffee is made from beans eaten and excreted by elephants. The fermentation process in the elephant's gut imparts a unique flavor.

29. **Airag (Mongolia):** Fermented horse milk, known as kumis in other regions, is a traditional Mongolian beverage. The fermentation gives it a slight alcoholic content and a sour taste.

30. **Huitlacoche (Mexico)**: Also known as corn smut or Mexican truffle, huitlacoche is a fungus that grows on corn kernels, considered a delicacy in Mexican cuisine, adding a mushroom-like flavor to dishes.

31. **Biltong (South Africa)**: Similar to jerky, biltong is dried, cured meat originating from South African countries. Unlike jerky, it's often made from various meats like beef or game, and seasoned with vinegar and spices.

32. **Geoduck (USA, Canada)**: A species of large saltwater clam with a long, protruding siphon. Geoduck is prized in seafood cuisine for its sweet, crunchy flesh, despite its unusual appearance.

33. **Pacha (Iraq):** A traditional dish made from boiled sheep's head, hooves, and stomachs, served with bread. It's considered a hearty breakfast meal and a cure for hangovers.

34. **Tea Eggs (China):** Hard-boiled eggs cracked slightly and then boiled again in tea, sauce, and spices. They have a marbled appearance and a savory flavor, commonly found as street food.

35. **Pemmican (North America):** A concentrated mixture of fat and protein used as a nutritious food historically by Indigenous peoples and later by the Arctic and Antarctic explorers.

36. **Awabi (Japan):** Abalone, a type of sea snail, is considered a delicacy in Japanese cuisine, often served raw or cooked in a variety of dishes. It's known for its tender texture and oceanic flavor.

37. **Lobster Ice Cream (USA):** A quirky dish from Maine, this ice cream incorporates cooked lobster meat into a butter-flavored base, challenging the traditional boundaries of sweet and savor y.

38. **Salmiakki (Finland):** A type of licorice flavored with ammonium chloride, giving it a strong, salty taste. This polarizing treat is beloved in Finland and other Nordic countries.

39. **Cobra Heart (Vietnam):** Consumed raw and still beating, cobra heart is a daring delicacy often served in a shot glass of the snake's blood. It's believed to impart strength and vitality.

40. **Yak Butter Tea (Tibet)**: A traditional Tibetan drink made by mixing tea with yak butter and salt. It's a staple in the Tibetan diet, providing essential nutrients in the harsh, high-altitude c lima te.

41. **Natto (Japan):** Fermented soybeans with a sticky texture and strong, cheese-like smell. Natto is a breakfast food in Japan, rich in protein and vitamins.

42. **Seal Flipper Pie (Canada):** A traditional Newfoundland dish, this pie is made with the flippers of harp seals, vegetables, and pastry. It's a source of controversy due to ethical concerns around seal hunting.

43. **Gỏi Cá (Vietnam):** A raw fish salad, similar to ceviche, seasoned with lime, chili, and various herbs. It reflects Vietnam's coastal culinary traditions.

44. **Kæstur Hákarl (Iceland):** Different from hákarl, kæstur hákarl specifically refers to the Greenland shark's fermented meat, known for its strong ammonia-rich smell and fishy taste.

45. **Pulque (Mexico):** An ancient alcoholic beverage made from the fermented sap of the agave plant. It dates back to Mesoamerican times and has a milky, slightly foamy texture.

46. **Fried Rattlesnake (USA**): Considered a delicacy in parts of the American Southwest, rattlesnake meat is often breaded and fried, described as tasting similar to frog legs or chicken.

47. **Bear Claw (North America):** A pastry that resembles a bear's paw, traditionally filled with almond paste and sometimes raisins. It's a nod to North American wildlife and a sweet treat.

48. **Durian Pizza (China):** Combining the potent smell and distinct taste of durian with pizza, this dish is a modern fusion that has gained popularity in parts of Asia.

49. **Squirrel Pie (UK):** Once a common dish in Britain, squirrel pie is made from the meat of grey squirrels. It's seen as a sustainable food source in areas where grey squirrels are overpopulated.

50. **Blood Tofu (China, Southeast Asia):** Made from coagulated pig or duck blood, cut into cubes and cooked in soups or stews. It's a traditional ingredient with a rich, metallic taste.

Chapter 6: Puzzles of the Universe

Section 6.1: Cosmic Mysteries

The universe is filled with mysteries that challenge our current understanding of physics, astronomy, and the nature of existence. From cosmic phenomena that defy explanation to enigmatic signals and uncharted cosmic territories, here are facts discussing some of the most perplexing unexplained phenomena in the universe:

1. **Dark Matter:** Comprising about 85% of the universe's mass, dark matter interacts with regular matter through gravity but does not emit, absorb, or reflect light, making it invisible and detectable only through its gravitational effects.

2. **Dark Energy:** A mysterious force that's driving the accelerated expansion of the universe, constituting about 68% of the universe's total energy. Its nature remains one of the biggest questions in cosmology.

3. **The Great Attractor:** A gravitational anomaly in intergalactic space that seems to be drawing the Milky Way and hundreds of thousands of other galaxies towards it with a gravitational force that cannot yet be explained by observed mass alone.

4. **Fast Radio Bursts (FRBs):** Intensely powerful bursts of radio waves from space that last only a few milliseconds. Their origins are unknown, with theories ranging from neutron stars to extraterrestrial intelligence.

5. **The Wow! Signal:** A strong narrowband radio signal received in 1977 by Ohio State University's Big Ear radio telescope. Thought by some to be of extraterrestrial origin, it has not been detected since.

6. **Neutron Stars Collision:** When two neutron stars collide, they can produce short gamma- ray bursts and heavy elements like gold and platinum, but the detailed mechanisms and aftermath are still being researched.

7. **KIC 8462852 (Tabby's Star):** Exhibits unusual light fluctuations, including significant dimming events. Various hypotheses have been proposed, including cometary fragments, planetary debris, and even alien megastructures.

8. **Antimatter:** While matter makes up most of the observable universe, antimatter is rare. The imbalance and the reason why our universe is made more of matter than antimatter is a major unsolved mystery.

9. **The Cosmic Microwave Background (CMB) Cold Spot:** An area of the CMB radiation that is significantly colder than the average, possibly indicating a vast area of the universe with a mass much lower than the norm.

10. **Galaxy Rotation Problem:** The outer stars of spiral galaxies rotate at the same rate as those near the center, contrary to what would be expected from Newtonian dynamics, suggesting the presence of dark matter.

11. **The Hubble Tension:** A discrepancy between the rate of the universe's expansion measured through observations of the early universe and the rate measured through local, later-time observations.

12. **Ultra-High-Energy Cosmic Rays:** Particles from space that strike the Earth's atmosphere with energies exceeding what theoretical physics can explain, challenging our understanding of cosmic ray sources and propagation.

13. **Mars Methane:** Methane detected on Mars varies seasonally and could imply biological activity or unknown geochemical processes, as methane on Earth is often produced by living organisms.

14. **The Pioneer Anomaly:** The unexplained deviations in the trajectories of the Pioneer 10 and 11 spacecraft, which seemed to indicate an additional, unaccounted-for sunward acceleration.

15. **The Galaxy's Missing Matter:** Observations suggest that galaxies contain less baryonic (ordinary) matter than expected from cosmological models, a discrepancy not fully explained by current theories.

16. **The Lithium Problem:** The observed abundance of lithium in the universe is significantly less than predicted by the Big Bang nucleosynthesis model, challenging our understanding of the early universe.

17. **The Venusian Anomaly:** Venus rotates on its axis very slowly and in the opposite direction to most planets in the solar system, a peculiar trait that has yet to be fully explained.

18. **The Kuiper Cliff**: The sudden drop-off in the number of objects observed beyond the edge of the Kuiper Belt, suggesting either an unknown gravitational influence or a different formation scenario for the solar system.

19. **Interstellar Object 'Oumuamua:** Its unusual acceleration as it passed through our solar system, along with its strange shape and rotation, has fueled speculation about its origin and na ture.

20. **The Void**: Vast regions of space that contain very few, if any, galaxies. The existence of these enormous voids is a challenge to current models of the universe's evolution.

21. **Black Hole Information Paradox:** The question of what happens to information that falls into a black hole, a problem that challenges principles of quantum mechanics and general relativity.

22. **White Holes:** Theoretical regions of space-time that cannot be entered from the outside, only exited. These are hypothetical opposites of black holes and remain purely speculative.

23. **Quantum Entanglement:** Described as "spooky action at a distance" by Einstein, it's the ability of particles to instantaneously correlate with each other regardless of distance, challenging classical notions of causality and locality.

24. The Fermi Paradox: The apparent contradiction between the high probability of extraterrestrial life and the lack of evidence for, or contact with such civilizations.

25. **The Planck Length:** The smallest length scale in the universe, beyond which classical ideas about gravity and space-time cease to be valid, and quantum effects dominate. The physical significance and implications of the Planck length remain speculative.

These phenomena underscore the vastness of our ignorance in the face of the universe's complexities, driving scientific inquiry and philosophical debate about the nature of reality.

Continuing our exploration into the enigmatic and unexplained phenomena of the universe, here are additional facts that highlight the depth of our curiosity and the limits of our understanding:

26. **Sonoluminescence:** A phenomenon where small gas bubbles in a liquid emit short bursts of light when subjected to intense sound waves. The precise mechanism behind the light emission remains unclear.

27. **Quantum Foam:** At the smallest scales, spacetime is believed to be frothy or foamy due to quantum fluctuations. This concept challenges our understanding of the fabric of the universe and how it behaves at quantum levels.

28. **The Alcubierre Drive:** A theoretical concept for faster-than-light travel that involves bending spacetime around a spacecraft. While it remains purely speculative, it poses questions about the possibilities of bending the rules of physics as we understand them.

29. **The Hexagon on Saturn:** A persisting hexagonal cloud pattern around the north pole of Saturn, with sides nearly 14,500 km (9,000 miles) long. The formation and stability of this hexagon are not fully understood.

30. **The Double-Slit Experiment:** Demonstrates that light and matter can display characteristics of both classically defined waves and particles, a fundamental concept in quantum mechanics that defies classical intuition.

31. **Magnetic Monopoles:** Theoretical particles that are magnets with only one pole, either a north or a south. Despite extensive searches, magnetic monopoles have not been observed, challenging theories of particle physics.

32. **The Eridanus Supervoid:** An unusually large region of space, nearly a billion light-years across, that contains very few galaxies. Its existence challenges current theories of the universe's structure.

33. **The Yarkovsky Effect:** A force acting on rotating bodies in space, caused by the anisotropic emission of thermal photons, which can alter asteroids' orbits over long periods. Its precise impacts on asteroid trajectories are complex and not fully predictable.

34. **Tetraneutrons:** A hypothetical particle made of four neutrons that, if it exists, would challenge the existing nuclear force theories since neutrons should repel each other in such close proximity.

35. **The Cyclic Model:** A cosmological model suggesting the universe undergoes endless cycles of Big Bangs and Big Crunches, challenging the one-time Big Bang theory. It raises questions about the nature of time and the universe's ultimate fate.

36. **Cold Fusion:** The controversial idea that nuclear fusion can occur at or near room temperature, which if possible, could revolutionize energy production. Despite occasional claims of success, reproducible results have eluded scientists.

37. **The Wow! Signal's Origin**: Beyond the initial speculation of extraterrestrial origin, the precise source of the Wow! The signal remains a mystery, with no repeat detections to help pinpoint its origin.

38. **Galactic Cannibalism:** The process by which large galaxies, including the Milky Way, grow by absorbing smaller galaxies. The detailed mechanics and outcomes of these cosmic meals are not fully understood.

39. **The Missing Baryon Problem**: Observations indicate that many of the universe's baryons (protons and neutrons) are missing from the visible universe, suggesting they are contained in hot, diffuse intergalactic gas clouds, yet direct detection remains elusive.

40. **Zombie Stars:** Stars that have gone supernova but appear to survive the explosion. These "zombie stars" challenge our understanding of star death and the conditions under which supernovae occur.

41. **The Anomalous Acceleration of the Universe:** The observation that the universe's expansion is accelerating is attributed to dark energy, but the nature of this acceleration and its long-term implications remain deeply mysterious.

42. **The Bootstrap Paradox in Cosmology:** A theoretical paradox where an object or information can exist without ever being created, through time travel or other means, challenging our understanding of causality and time.

43. **The Multiverse Theory:** Suggests the existence of multiple or even an infinite number of universes beyond our own, each with different physical constants and laws of physics, a concept that remains speculative without empirical evidence.

44. **Quantum Tunneling:** A phenomenon where particles pass through barriers that would be insurmountable according to classical physics. It plays a crucial role in nuclear fusion in stars but challenges our macroscopic understanding of barriers.

45. **The Information Loss Paradox in Black Holes**: Suggests that physical information could permanently disappear in a black hole, clashing with the principle of quantum determinism, which posits that future states of a system are determined by its initial conditions.

46. **The Reionization Epoch:** A period in the universe's early history when the first stars and galaxies ionized the intergalactic medium. Details about what caused this, how it progressed, and its implications for cosmic structure formation remain uncertain.

47. **Galactic Superwaves:** Hypothetical waves of energy that travel through galaxies, potentially initiated by supermassive black hole activities or starburst phenomena. Their existence and impact on galaxy evolution are not yet proven.

48. **The Baryogenesis Problem:** The observed imbalance between matter and antimatter in the universe. Current theories cannot fully explain why the Big Bang produced more matter than antimatter, allowing the universe as we know it to exist.

49. **The Singularity Problem in General Relativity:** Predicts that spacetime curvatures become infinite in black holes, challenging our understanding of physics at extreme conditions and the need for a quantum theory of gravity.

50. **Ultra-Diffuse Galaxies:** Ghostly galaxies with very few stars but as large as the Milky Way. Their formation, stability, and the role of dark matter in their structure are not fully understood.

These mysteries underscore the vastness of our universe and the continuous quest for knowledge that drives scientific discovery and theoretical innovation. Each unexplained phenomenon represents a puzzle piece in the vast, intricate mosaic of the cosmos.

Section 6.2: Theories of Time and Space

Exploring concepts that challenge our understanding of reality takes us into the realms of quantum mechanics, cosmology, philosophy, and beyond. These ideas push the boundaries of what we consider possible and question the very fabric of our existence. Here are facts about concepts that stretch, and sometimes shatter, our conventional views of reality:

1. **Quantum Superposition:** Particles can exist in multiple states simultaneously until observed, challenging the classical idea that objects have a definite state at all times.

2. **Simulation Theory:** The hypothesis that our reality might be an advanced digital simulation run by a more sophisticated civilization. It questions the nature of existence and reality itself.

3. **Nonlocality:** Quantum entanglement suggests that particles can be connected in such a way that the state of one (no matter the distance) can instantly affect the state of another, defying classical ideas of space and time.

4. **Many-Worlds Interpretation:** A theory in quantum mechanics proposing that all possible alternate histories and futures are real, each representing an actual "world" or universe.

5. **Consciousness as a Fundamental Aspect of Reality:** Some theories propose that consciousness is not a byproduct of the brain but a fundamental feature of the universe, challenging materialistic views of consciousness.

6. **Holographic Principle:** The idea that all the information contained within a volume of space can be represented as a hologram—a two-dimensional surface that encodes the three-dimensional data.

7. **Time Dilation:** According to the theory of relativity, time moves slower for an object in motion compared to one at rest. This has been confirmed by experiments, challenging our intuitive understanding of time.

8. **Plato's Theory of Forms:** Suggests that the physical world is not as real or true as timeless, absolute ideas called forms, challenging perceptions of physical reality and suggesting a higher level of existence.

9. **The Observer Effect:** The act of observation can alter the outcome of a quantum experiment, suggesting that the observer plays a vital role in the behavior of physical systems.

10. **Tachyons:** Hypothetical particles that travel faster than light, which, if they exist, could potentially send information backward in time, challenging causality.

11. **Quantum Zeno Effect:** The phenomenon whereby a quantum system can be frozen in its state by measuring it frequently enough, challenging the notion that quantum processes are continuous and unaffected by observation.

12. **The Anthropic Principle:** The idea that the universe is fine-tuned to allow for the existence of life, or that observations of the universe must be compatible with the conscious life that observes it.

13. **Quantum Decoherence:** The process by which quantum systems interact with their environments to exhibit probabilistically additive behavior, leading to the classical world we observe, challenging the clear division between the quantum and classical worlds.

14. **Panpsychism:** The theory that consciousness is a fundamental and ubiquitous aspect of the physical world, suggesting that all matter has consciousness.

15. **Block Universe Theory:** Proposes that past, present, and future exist simultaneously in a four-dimensional block, challenging our experience of time as flowing from past to future.

16. **Quantum Tunneling:** Particles can pass through barriers that they classically shouldn't be able to surmount, a principle used in modern electronics but puzzling from a classical physics standpoint.

17. **The Bootstrap Paradox:** A theoretical paradox where an object or piece of information can exist without ever being created through time travel, challenging linear concepts of time and causality.

18. **The Mandela Effect**: A phenomenon where a large group of people remembers an event or detail differently from how it occurred, leading some to speculate about alternate realities or universes.

19. **Quantum Immortality**: A thought experiment in quantum mechanics suggesting that the observer continues to exist in a parallel universe when faced with a life-threatening event, challenging the notions of life and death.

20. **Chaos Theory:** The principle that small changes in the initial conditions of a complex system can have large effects, challenging the predictability of deterministic systems.

21. **Biocentrism:** The idea that life creates the universe rather than the opposite, suggesting that consciousness shapes the physical world around us.

22. **The Double-Slit Experiment's Implications:** Demonstrates that particles behave differently when observed, challenging the classical idea of an objective reality.

23. **Quantum Entropy:** This suggests that information could be a fundamental component of the universe, challenging traditional notions of thermodynamics and information loss.

24. **The Problem of Free Will in Quantum Mechanics:** Quantum indeterminacy suggests that determinism is not absolute, providing a potential quantum foundation for the concept of free will.

25. **Neuroplasticity and Reality Perception:** The brain's ability to reorganize itself by forming new neural connections throughout life, suggests that our perception of reality can change based on our thoughts and experiences.

These concepts, drawn from various scientific and philosophical disciplines, encourage us to question our preconceived notions of reality.

Continuing with the exploration of profound concepts that stretch the boundaries of our understanding of reality, here are additional facts delving deeper into mysteries and theories that challenge conventional thought:

26. **Zero-Point Energy:** The lowest possible energy that a quantum mechanical system may have, implying that empty space is filled with energy. This challenges classical notions of a vacuum and could have implications for the future of energy technology.

27. **Quantum Backflow:** A phenomenon where particles moving in one direction can temporarily exhibit a flow of probability in the opposite direction, defying classical expectations of motion.

28. **Delayed Choice Quantum Eraser:** An experiment that suggests actions in the present can influence events in the past, on a quantum level, challenging our linear understanding of time.

29. **Quantum Entanglement in Time:** The idea that particles can be entangled not just in space but across time, suggests a more complex interconnection of events than previously thought.

30. **Quantum Biology:** The study of quantum phenomena in biological systems, such as photosynthesis and bird navigation, suggesting that quantum mechanics plays a role in life processes.

31. **The Fine-Tuned Universe**: The observation that certain fundamental physical constants are precisely set for life to exist, leading to speculation about the anthropic principle and the possibility of a multiverse.

32. **The Twin Paradox:** A thought experiment in special relativity where one twin who travels at high speed ages slower than the twin who remains on Earth, challenging our understanding of time and aging.

33. **Quantum Vacuum Fluctuations:** The temporary appearance of energetic particles out of nothing, as allowed by the Heisenberg uncertainty principle, challenging the concept of a true vacuum.

34. **The Fermi Paradox and the Great Filter:** The contradiction between the high probability of extraterrestrial life and the lack of contact with such civilizations, suggests we might not understand life's rarity or the barriers to its persistence.

35. **The Black Hole Information Paradox:** Suggests information could be lost in black holes, conflicting with quantum theory, which states that information cannot be destroyed.

36. **The Hard Problem of Consciousness:** The question of why and how subjective experiences arise from physical processes in the brain, challenging our understanding of consciousness.

37. **Quantum Suicide and Immortality:** A thought experiment suggesting that the observer will always find themselves alive in one branch of the multiverse, touching on the intersection of quantum mechanics and the philosophy of death.

38. **The Arrow of Time:** The one-way direction or asymmetry of time, which is not directly apparent in the laws of physics, leads to questions about why time seems to move forward and not backward.

39. **Non-Euclidean Geometry:** Geometry that doesn't hold the parallel postulate of Euclidean geometry, suggesting the fabric of space may not be flat but curved, influencing our understanding of space and the universe.

40. **The Unobservable Universe:** Parts of the universe are beyond our observable horizon due to the finite speed of light and the expansion of the universe, suggesting there are aspects of reality we may never know.

41. **Dark Flow:** The unexplained phenomenon where galaxy clusters appear to be moving at high speeds along a common direction, suggesting influences beyond the observable universe.

42. **The Multiverse Hypothesis in Philosophy:** The idea that there could be many universes with different versions of ourselves, challenging our understanding of existence and identity.

43. **The Measurement Problem in Quantum Mechanics:** The problem of how (or whether) wave function collapse occurs, leading to questions about the role of observation and measurement in reality.

44. **The Global Consciousness Project:** An experiment suggesting that human consciousness can affect the behavior of random number generators, implying a form of global consciousness interconnection.

45. **Panpsychism and Integrated Information Theory (IIT):** Theories suggesting consciousness arises from the integration of information, which could imply that all systems possess some level of consciousness.

46. **Quantum Gravity:** The search for a theory that combines quantum mechanics and general relativity, challenging our understanding of the universe's most fundamental forces.

47. **The Poincaré Recurrence Theorem:** The theorem suggests that certain systems will return to a state very close to their initial state, challenging our notions of entropy and the irreversibility of time.

48. **The Gödel Incompleteness Theorems:** Proofs that in any sufficiently complex system, there are statements that are true but cannot be proven within the system, challenging the completeness and consistency of mathematical systems.

49. **The Boltzmann Brain Hypothesis:** Suggests that it is more likely for a single brain to spontaneously and temporarily arise in a state of entropy than for a whole universe to do so, challenging our assumptions about the nature of our existence.

50. **The No-Cloning Theorem in Quantum Mechanics:** States it is impossible to create an exact copy of an arbitrary unknown quantum state, challenging concepts of identity and replication at a quantum level.

These concepts continue to perplex and fascinate scientists, philosophers, and the curious mind, pushing the boundaries of what we know and understand about the universe and our place within it.

Section 6.3: <u>Future Technologies and Exploration</u>

Speculating on the future of human technology and space travel involves imagining the boundaries of innovation, exploration, and our quest for knowledge. Here are facts that explore potential advancements and milestones we may achieve in the realms of technology and space exploration:

1. **Quantum Computing:** Future quantum computers could solve problems in seconds that current supercomputers couldn't solve in thousands of years, revolutionizing fields from cryptography to drug discovery.

2. **Space Elevators**: Carbon nanotubes or other advanced materials could enable the construction of space elevators, dramatically reducing the cost of transporting materials and people to space.

3. **Terraforming Mars:** Advances in technology may one day allow us to alter the Martian environment to make it habitable for humans, possibly using genetically engineered microbes to produce a breathable atmosphere.

4. **Fusion Power:** If controlled fusion power is achieved, it would provide a nearly limitless, clean energy source, potentially solving many of Earth's energy challenges and powering future space missions.

5. **Interstellar Travel:** Breakthroughs in propulsion technology, such as the theoretical Alcubierre drive, could one day enable us to travel to nearby star systems within human lifetimes.

6. **Brain-Computer Interfaces (BCIs):** Future BCIs could enhance human cognitive abilities, allow for telepathic communication, and enable direct control of technology with thought.

7. **Autonomous Vehicles:** Widespread adoption of autonomous vehicles could transform transportation, reducing accidents caused by human error and optimizing traffic flow.

8. **Artificial General Intelligence (AGI):** The development of AGI, machines with the ability to understand or learn any intellectual task that a human being can, could redefine our relationship with technology.

9. **Dyson Spheres:** Advanced civilizations could construct Dyson spheres, megastructures that encompass a star to capture its power output, providing immense energy resources.

10. **Nanotechnology**: Advances in nanotechnology could lead to medical nanobots that repair damage at the cellular level, smart materials that adapt to their environment, and more efficient energy storage systems.

11. **Colonizing the Solar System:** The future may see humans establishing colonies on the Moon, Mars, and even in the asteroid belt, exploiting local resources for expansion and sur vival.

12. **3D Printing of Organs:** Advancements in 3D bioprinting could make organ transplants more accessible by creating organs on demand, potentially ending the organ shortage crisis.

13. **The Singularity:** The point at which technological growth becomes uncontrollable and irreversible, potentially resulting in unfathomable changes to human civilization, could be reached through the development of AGI.

14. **Wireless Power Transmission:** The future may bring widespread wireless power, eliminating the need for batteries and power cords and enabling new forms of mobile technology.

15. **Personalized Medicine:** Advances in genomics and biotechnology could lead to highly personalized medical treatments tailored to each individual's genetic makeup, significantly increasing treatment efficacy.

16. **Virtual Reality (VR) and Augmented Reality (AR):** Future VR and AR technologies could become indistinguishable from reality, profoundly impacting entertainment, education, and social interactions.

17. **Space-based Solar Power:** Collecting solar power in space and wirelessly transmitting it to Earth could provide an unlimited supply of clean energy, reducing our dependence on fossil fuels.

18. **Asteroid Mining:** The extraction of valuable materials from asteroids could provide a new economic boom, supplying rare metals for electronics, construction materials for space

habitats, and water for life support and fuel.

19. **Artificial Photosynthesis:** Scientists are working on artificial photosynthesis systems that could efficiently produce fuels from sunlight, carbon dioxide, and water, mimicking plants but at a much larger scale.

20. **Digital Immortality**: Advances in neuroscience and computing might enable the upload of human consciousness to computers, allowing for a form of immortality.

21. **Anti-aging Therapies:** Ongoing research into the biology of aging could lead to effective therapies for extending the human lifespan significantly, possibly allowing people to live healthily for centuries.

22. **Universal Translators**: Real-time, highly accurate translation devices could eliminate language barriers, fostering global communication and understanding.

23. **Cloaking Devices:** Research into metamaterials may lead to the development of cloaking devices that can render objects invisible or undetectable to certain forms of detection.

24. **Self-replicating Machines:** Machines capable of replicating themselves from raw materials could be used for large-scale construction projects in space, such as building habitats or mining operations.

25. **The Galactic Internet:** The development of a communication network that spans the solar system, or even reaches into interstellar space, could allow for the transfer of data between Earth and distant colonies or spacecraft.

These speculative advancements highlight the potential for human ingenuity to overcome current limitations and open new frontiers in technology and space exploration.

Continuing to delve into the realm of future possibilities, here are more speculative facts on the horizon of human technology and space travel, envisioning the next leaps forward in our quest to redefine the boundaries of innovation and exploration:

26. **Ultra-Fast Hyperloops:** Proposing to transport people and goods at speeds exceeding 700 miles per hour in near-vacuum tubes, hyperloops could revolutionize terrestrial transportation, making cross-continental travel as quick as a subway ride.

27. **Space Tourism:** Beyond brief suborbital flights, space tourism could expand to include orbital hotels, lunar vacations, and even guided tours of asteroids, making space travel accessible to more than just astronauts.

28. **Neuromorphic Computing:** Inspired by the human brain, neuromorphic chips could lead to computers that can process information more efficiently than traditional systems, revolutionizing AI and machine learning.

29. **Deep Sea Cities:** As terrestrial space becomes scarce, humanity could look to the oceans for new living spaces, constructing underwater habitats that harness the sea's resources for energy and food.

30. **Smart Dust:** Tiny, sensor-laden devices that can float in the air, monitor environmental data, track movements, or even conduct espionage, could become a pervasive part of our environment.

31. **Genetic Engineering of Humans:** Advanced CRISPR technology and gene editing could lead to the elimination of hereditary diseases, extended lifespans, and enhanced human abilities.

32. **Lunar Solar Power:** The Moon's surface, constantly exposed to sunlight in certain regions, could host solar farms that beam energy back to Earth, providing a constant and vast energy supply.

33. **Augmented Reality (AR) Contact Lenses**: AR contact lenses could project data and imagery directly into the wearer's field of vision, blending digital information with the physical world seamlessly.

34. **Atmospheric Water Generation:** Advanced technologies could efficiently extract large quantities of water from the atmosphere, providing fresh water to arid regions and revolutionizing water distribution.

35. **Quantum Internet**: Utilizing quantum entanglement for data transmission, a quantum internet could provide unhackable communication channels, fundamentally changing online security and information sharing.

36. **Plasma Shields:** Research into plasma physics could lead to the development of plasma-based shields, protecting astronauts from harmful cosmic radiation and enabling safer long-duration space missions.

37. **Mass Driver Launch Systems:** Electromagnetic catapults, or mass drivers, could launch spacecraft and cargo off the Moon or other bodies with weak gravity, reducing the need for chemical rockets.

38. **Orbital Ring Space Elevator:** An advancement over the space elevator concept, an orbital ring could encircle the entire Earth, serving as a base for elevators ascending into space from multiple points.

39. **Zero-waste Closed-loop Systems:** Future habitats in space and on Earth could achieve zero-waste status through closed-loop systems that recycle and reuse all resources, vital for sustainable living off-planet.

40. **Autonomous Construction Robots**: Robots capable of autonomous construction could build habitats on Mars or the Moon before human arrival, preparing safe dwellings and infrastructure for colonists.

41. **Phased-array Optics:** Advanced telescopes with phased-array optics could observe planets in distant solar systems in great detail, identifying signs of life or suitable conditions for habitation.

42. **Cryonics and Revival Technologies:** The refinement of cryonics could lead to the preservation of human life for revival in the future, potentially offering a form of immortality or extended space travel.

43. **Smart Materials:** Materials that can change their properties on demand, such as shape, color, or conductivity, could lead to revolutionary applications in manufacturing, wearables, and construction.

44. **Interplanetary Internet:** Developing a reliable interplanetary communication network could enable internet access on Mars and other celestial bodies, supporting the needs of future colonies.

45. **AI Governance:** The integration of advanced AI systems in governance could optimize decision-making processes, improve public services, and personalize education and healthcare services.

46. **Nanorobotics in Medicine:** Nanorobots can perform precise surgeries at the cellular level, deliver drugs directly to target cells, and continuously monitor health from within the body.

47. **Gravitational Wave Astronomy:** As detection methods improve, gravitational wave observatories could provide new insights into the cosmos, including the behavior of black holes and the nature of dark matter.

48. **Bio-regenerative Life Support Systems:** Systems that mimic Earth's natural cycles could support long-term space missions, recycling waste and producing food and oxygen via plants and microorganisms.

49. **Astroengineering Megastructures:** Future civilizations could construct megastructures like Dyson swarms or Shkadov thrusters, harnessing the energy of stars or gradually shifting stellar orbits.

50. **Teleportation of Information:** While teleporting matter remains a distant dream, the teleportation of information via quantum entanglement could revolutionize communication, leading to instantaneous data transfer across vast distances.

These speculations paint a picture of a future where human ingenuity and technology have transformed not only how we live on Earth but also how we interact with the cosmos, forever altering our place in the universe.

Conclusion

When we come to the end of our "eternal quest" it is necessary to stop and think about the journey we have taken together. By exploring countless topics, from the mysteries of the universe to the paradoxes of human consciousness, we reach far beyond the known, driven by humanity (often curiosity). Curiosity, the desire to understand the world around us, has pushed humans forward since the dawn of humanity. It is the fire that burns in the heart of every child who wonders about the stars, it is the fire that burns in the heart of every scientist

who questions the limits of reality, and it is the fire that burns in the heart of everyone who stops wondering. from the beauty of the natural world. This book is a meditation on the insatiable thirst for knowledge, a celebration of unanswered questions, and an acknowledgment of mysteries forever beyond our reach. But knowledge is more than just finding answers. It's about learning to ask better questions. It's about understanding that with every discovery the unknown horizon recedes, and new mysteries emerge just waiting for us to discover. This endless cycle is not a Sisyphus-specific situation, but a situation full of curiosity and joy. It reminds us that the universe is more complex and beautiful than we think. When we close this chapter, I want you to think about the beginning, not the end. The journey of discovery and discovery does not end on the last page of a book; It is an endless journey that we must all undertake if we want to truly live, not just live. The world around us is full of wonders waiting to be discovered, questions waiting to be asked, and mysteries waiting to be solved. Follow your instincts, let them guide your steps, and don't worry about where they will lead. To my readers who are with me on this journey, know that your curiosity is the most powerful tool you can use. This is not only the key to unlocking the secrets of the world, but also the key to unlocking your own unlimited potential. Therefore, let us promise to never forget our thirst for knowledge, and to always approach the world with the enthusiasm and enthusiasm of an explorer adventuring into the unknown and the curiosity and admiration it deserves. After all, our eternal quest for knowledge is not just a search for answers, but also a love of the questions themselves. It is a testament to our indomitable spirit, our relentless drive to transcend understanding, and our endless journey into the unknown. Just ask. Go look for it. Have a dream. Because the journey in pursuit of wisdom is a journey we all take together, guided by the wonder of the universe and the wonder of the human spirit.

9 798322 193319